CONTENTS

INTRODUCTION

The purpose of this book is for you to write your first song. That's it? Yes it is.

Not just any song, of course, but one you are proud of, one that gives you the confidence and the process you need to write your second, third, and on and on. Like anything, the difference between zero and one is enormous. With zero you have nothing; with one you have something: a start. Writing songs is the same. Think of that number as your self-esteem or confidence as a songwriter. With just one song you start to get positive results, and after that the number keeps increasing. Someone who has never written a song might want to be a songwriter, but someone who has written one is a songwriter.

Your first song is the hardest one you will ever write.

There are all sorts of reasons that keep even great musicians from writing a single song. You might be a great player, terrific singer, superb improviser, and killer interpreter, and yet freeze up when staring at that blank page of manuscript paper or computer screen. It may seem impossible because you think you need to be inspired and have great ideas fall into your head from some magical place. You may think your musical heroes are geniuses who can write songs, and that you are not. Perhaps they are geniuses, but they have something else you can share: knowledge of the *craft* of writing a song. Inspiration may come to us in different degrees and at different times, but the ability to keep writing even without it is dedication to working at your craft. It is work, but it's enjoyable work. The more you work at it, the more often you will find that inspiration "just happens."

This book will give you two things: the basic musical *knowledge* you need to write a song, and a *process* for putting that knowledge to work. The musical knowledge may seem basic, and you may already have all or most of it, but our perspective on it will be one that is most useful for creating a song. This involves looking at musical materials differently from a classical composer, or music analyst, or critic, or theorist: the audience that most music theory books are written for. The material needed to write a song is not that complex, but even a small gap can stifle a creative idea or kill a song that has potential. Maybe you have tried to write before; maybe you've written a song but still don't "feel" like a songwriter. This book will change your mind as it changes your view of musical material and your approach to writing a song with it.

This is where process comes in. While you may refine your process over the years, and hone it as you gain experience, you need one to begin with that suits your working style, and that produces results for you. I will not tell you what works for me; we will find what works for you. You will know that it works because you will have tangible proof: your first song.

I would be a terrible baseball coach if I told you to hit a home run your first time at bat. My goal is to show you how to get on base first, to get into the game and then improve. Once you have started writing songs you are proud of, you can search out books or a teacher to help you improve certain areas where you need help, but as a beginner you need specific assistance. You do not need to be told the nuances of power-slugging before you know how to hold the bat properly, yet there are dozens of books (at least) that approach songwriting that way, purporting to get you into the Top 40 or win a Grammy by using their approach. Even the best writers did not begin like this. To improve as a writer you need to have something to improve on, and as a songwriter that means your own songs. Once you have your first song done to your satisfaction and have a basic process to help you write more, you can start improving your songwriting. In fact, you can use the techniques we will be using to improve your first attempts to improve your later songs. But first things first.

Let's make *you* into a songwriter.

Write Your First Song

By Dr. Dave Walker

To access audio visit:
www.halleonard.com/mylibrary

Enter Code
3301-0118-9246-6085

ISBN 978-1-4950-0193-2

HAL•LEONARD®
CORPORATION

7777 W. BLUEMOUND RD. P.O. BOX 13819 MILWAUKEE, WI 53213

In Australia Contact:
Hal Leonard Australia Pty. Ltd.
4 Lentara Court
Cheltenham, Victoria, 3192 Australia
Email: ausadmin@halleonard.com.au

Visit Hal Leonard Online at
www.halleonard.com

OUR AIMS

1. The big one is to get you over the hump of wanting to write a song but not doing it.
2. Discover a process that works for you.
3. Find and develop your strengths.
4. Find and fix your weaker areas.
5. Find out if songwriting is for you.
6. Give you the confidence to keep going.

WHAT YOU NEED TO USE THIS BOOK

You need a way to keep and organize your ideas and finished songs. Being able to write music in the treble clef is ideal, but even if you can you should still have a recorder close at hand and a pad to write lyric ideas on when they come to you, at any time of day or night. You need to keep track of these to retrieve them later.

You should be able to play an instrument that can produce chords (several notes at once), such as guitar, harp, banjo, autoharp, piano, organ, synthesizer, accordion, or any other keyboard instrument.

Ideally you should be able to sing well enough to line out your own melody, if only in the shower for yourself. If not, you should use your recorder (or recording software) to play your melody along with the chords that accompany it. It is essential that you hear your words and melody along with the chords.

That's all. We will be aiming to write your first song as a "lead sheet," which will contain the melody, lyrics, and chord names. If you can't write music, place the chords over the lyrics and make an accurate recording. If you are an accomplished player and want to include a more complex accompaniment, that's fine. However, except in certain situations, which we will look at later, you can simply specify the chords by name.

Don't worry about any gaps in your knowledge of music theory, harmony, or even melody writing. Use the appendices at the back of this book for a quick overview or refresher on important aspects of music – and even extra material to extend your ideas. You don't need to master all of these, but they are there if you need them or are just interested in learning more.

THE ONE AND ONLY RULE

You need to be free to experiment and try out as many things as you like, so we'll give you guidelines and pointers rather than rules. If you have a better idea, try it first. If it doesn't work, try mine and see what the difference is. But our one rule is for your own protection, and that of your song: *Do not sing your song for anyone until it is finished!*

There is nothing so deflating as an uncomprehending stare from someone you hope to impress with your song. I have seen too many budding writers just give up because a loved one failed to be swept off their feet by an early draft of what could have turned out to be a fine song. What happened?

As the writer, you can hear "into" the song. You know what you meant to say, rather than what you actually said. You mentally fill in gaps with a brilliant accompaniment, or hear your favorite singer belting out the tune with a full band and orchestra. You know that it is a first draft, but you are imagining the final result. On the other side, your listener is hearing it for the first time, may not even catch all the words, may prefer or expect a different style, and most of all hears it as a finished song meant to compete with all-time classics. It is the perfect setup for miscommunication and hurt feelings.

Once you have finished it, you will have a better idea of your song's virtues and faults, and you will be capable of directing your listener to its finer points and your intentions, as well as taking any criticism with confidence. You might even decide to keep your first song for yourself, a trophy of your new ability. As a songwriter, that's your right.

CHAPTER 1
GETTING STARTED

HOW TO USE THIS BOOK

This book is set up in two ways. You may want to use it to guide you through writing your first song, in which case there are suggestions at the end of each chapter for applying its ideas and techniques to your song. It is also designed as a reference, so that you can return to any chapter to review the ideas on a particular aspect of songwriting. The chapters are pretty much stand-alone, so you can read them in the order you wish (there will be some repetition of information to accommodate it). They are "pretty much stand-alone" since, as you will see, all aspects of a song are related and so no one part is isolated from the whole.

TWO GUIDING PRINCIPLES

Before we even start, there are two principles that will show up in everything we do. They will appear in different forms, but they boil down to: similarity and difference. They will appear as repetition and variation, consistency and contrast, consonance and dissonance, and others we will discuss when we get to them. All music is a fine balance between keeping things similar enough so that your listener can follow you and different enough to keep them interested. The balance shifts quite a bit between genres of music – say, between a simple country ballad and an avant-garde string quartet – but the background ideas remain the same.

WHEN TO START

Now. There is no greater enemy of creativity than procrastination. "Let me put that on my calendar for tomorrow and I'll get to it if I can." Yeah, right. The best thing you could do is put this book down and start to write right now. But since I do not believe in rules I can hardly make that a rule, and since we don't want to be dogmatic I'll allow that it would be a good idea to finish reading this chapter on getting started, and *then* starting immediately. If you wait for "inspiration to strike" or even "an idea to come to you," you may be waiting a long time. Working at songwriting will bring out a lot of ideas; some of them will be good, a few first-rate. Some lucky few have a great idea early in their career, others go through a lot of lousy ideas before brilliance strikes. Chet Atkins was "amazed at how the most talented people seem to be the ones that work the hardest." Bach once said that anyone who worked as hard as he did would achieve similar results –overly modest perhaps, but a valid relation between work and musical excellence.

Although it might seem a bit far afield from writing popular songs today, a quick look at the sketches that Beethoven made for some of his most famous works can be startling. The ordinary, boring, almost inane ideas that he begins with can be a shock, as are the dozens of pages of variations as he slowly develops this ludicrously simple idea into more and more powerful expressions until they finally shape into a symphony that astonishes listeners hundreds of years later. This from a man regarded by many as the most brilliant composer ever to have lived! He managed this by studying his craft and working at set hours every day, making it a habit he practiced his entire life. And in case you have the wrong impression, he was actually a pretty average student of music theory, not outstanding in any way. He kept most of his exercises from his student days, and they are riddled with blatant mistakes. So learn from your mistakes and keep working!

A SPECIAL NOTE TO ACCOMPLISHED SONGWRITERS

What accomplished songwriter would read a book on writing a first song when they already have several under their belt? A wise one. Many Zen-based activities, including martial arts, emphasize the need for a "beginner's mind" in approaching the goal. If you are too sophisticated in your thinking or too impressed with your accomplishments, you can miss the subtlety and beauty that brought you to songwriting in the first place. This book can help you remember the rudiments you have forgotten and yet are still basic to your art. We may be impressed by displays of flash and complexity, but remember how astonishing it is to be deeply moved by something so simple that "anyone could have thought of that" – but no one else did. From time to time, we need to recall the thrill of the first time we played a chord on a guitar, struck a key on a piano, sang a song we loved – when we connected with music in the special way that makes a musician and not just a listener.

I'm not a Zen master, but I do believe in the wisdom of returning to the basics every few years, especially when I feel jaded or stuck for ideas. Students and colleagues are often shocked to see a beginner's manual on my stand or desk, but as I explain I'm not looking for what I don't know. Rather, I'm searching for what I do know but have forgotten or am not using. Have I really exhausted all the basic materials of music? Has anyone?

HOW SONGWRITERS LISTEN TO SONGS

Listening to your favorite songs and calling it work is one of the perks of being a songwriter. One of the secrets of the great songwriters is that they make it work, pleasant work though it is. You can use this technique to personalize this book. Listen to your favorite songs and make a note of each spot that really connects with you, then go back and figure out why. Either stop the song at that spot or write it down, but do not count on your memory. Your favorite songwriters are teaching you lessons. These are definitely classes you don't want to skip!

Take the time you need to figure out what affected you: a word, a chord, the motion of a melody, a verbal image. All these can create the germs of ideas you can expand upon in your own songs. This is work, though, and you will often have to dig deep to understand exactly what you are hearing. For example, you may hear a chord that knocks you out, but when you play it yourself it seems ordinary. Maybe it is how it is placed in the progression, perhaps unexpected at this point. In another case, an upbeat song might have just a short twinge of sadness that strikes you as unusually poignant. Your reaction is telling you that whatever is happening is effective. If it worked for someone else, you can make it work for you. The idea is not to use it in the same way – that's already been done – but to find a way to do something similar, and maybe even more convincingly, in your own way.

We will discuss many ways to achieve this as we go on, but for starters let's consider a song that catches your attention with a sad minor chord during an otherwise happy, celebratory chorus. Maybe it strikes you as a reminder that life is short, or that every life is clouded by misfortune, or even that the success the song celebrates is short-lived. Any of these could become the basis for an entire song of yours, while the original idea was just a suggestion. Or maybe you are writing a similar sort of happy song, but have been stuck for a chorus idea; this might suggest going in a different direction in the chorus.

Take the general idea and make it personal by stating it in your own way. A good frame of mind is "How can I make this more [whatever the influence is]"? How can you make your chord progression even more surprising? How can the contrast in your lyrics be even more effective? How can your melody build to an even greater climax?

WAYS TO GET STARTED WRITING

There are many ways to get started writing a song. Let's examine the most common ones. If you don't have an idea you are itching to turn into a song, give each of these a try and see which you like:

- Start with a song title.

- Start with a situation you know well and feel strongly about.

- Start with a phrase that strikes you as meaningful.

- Fool around on your instrument until you come across a phrase you like.

- Use a chord progression you really like.

Start with a song title

A good title can give you great ideas for lyrics and suggest a type of music to accompany it. Occasionally, a person will say something that strikes you, as when John Lennon was struck by a remark Ringo made and thus came up with the title "A Hard Day's Night" for the Beatles. George Harrison picked random words from a book to get "gently" and "weeps," which became "While My Guitar Gently Weeps." This in turn suggested Eric Clapton's iconic solo of a weeping guitar. Odd phrases can call up unique ideas. Years ago, after a week of sun showers, I heard myself tell a friend "It Only Rains When the Sun Is Out," which I used as the title of my next song.

One word of warning. Many people will tell you that a song title cannot be copyrighted. While generally true, it is still a terrible idea to choose an iconic song title for your new composition. That type of muddle will never help your song. If you decided to call your song "Yesterday," confusion with the massive hit would be made worse by the inevitable comparison of your song to a classic. It can, however, be a good starting point to get you thinking of what was meaningful to you about yesterday – perhaps "Yesterday When We Met" or "Yesterday You Left" or "Yesterday, My Lucky Day." The title, lyrics, and music work together to either reinforce one another (similarity) or conflict (difference). So "Yesterday, My Lucky Day" could be a story of love found and then lost, so that it changes from happy to sad, and the title then becomes ironic.

Start with a situation you know well and feel strongly about

Many songs are written when the writer falls into or out of love. People never tire of good love songs, even sad ones, because they can relate to them. It is crucial that your situation be both personal for you and yet widely shared, so that people feel it includes them. Loss of your pet hamster may be devastating for you, but hard to communicate to the majority of people. The loss of a close friend, on the other hand is something that we all know. Changing your approach to the subject and keeping it more general allows you to express yourself personally while including others, who may have a different experience in mind for the same emotions. Who knows that "Goodbye, Dexter" is really about your pet hamster?

Start with a phrase that strikes you as meaningful

A songwriter should always be listening for phrases that sound like lyrics, because they can come from anywhere at any time. Carry a small pad and pencil with you to collect these gems that are too easily forgotten. Someone might say "If I had yesterday back again…" or "She looks fine, but yesterday…" or even a twisted cliché like "Nice weather we're not having." Anything that starts to fire your imagination can be a good start. Be careful not to immediately reject something on "second thought." If it struck you, there is a good chance it will strike many listeners. At least give it a chance. The more of these you gather, the better the chances of finding a great one, and the keener your ear will get. (See my real-life example on page 14.)

Fool around on your instrument until you come across a phrase you like

Especially when things are hectic, it can be therapeutic to fool around on your instrument, playing whatever comes into your mind without a plan, just for the fun of it. When you stumble across something you like, make a note of it: Write it down or record it on your phone or mp3 player and see where it takes you. You do not have to start with words; sometimes a good melody will suggest words to go with it. Paul McCartney wrote the melody for "Yesterday" before he had even the first word. (The temporary words he used, "Scrambled eggs," fit the accent pattern of the first three notes, but not the feel of the song.) Try new things rather than the same places your fingers tend to go when you play. There is no right or wrong here. You are trying to find something that pleases you at this point, something you would like to make even better. Record these sessions or you will forget the really good ideas you come up with.

Use a chord progression you really like

This is most useful when you come across a series of chords that strike your ear as new and interesting. Try to avoid clichés, since your listeners will hear them coming and have heard them too often before. Many songs hold a chord over a descending bass line, so if your bass line descends, try to change chords above it. A minor chord with a chromatically descending bass was an R&B standard well before McCartney used it in "Got to Get You Into My Life;" he used it specifically for the clichéd effect. George Harrison modified its effect in "Something" by moving the descending line into the middle of the chord, which he modified to A major. "Stairway to Heaven" begins with the same progression, again using a minor chord, but with a distinctive guitar part that changes the second and fourth chords. While the background harmonic idea is similar, the effects are different because of important modifications. We might sum these up by saying that a background idea can be similar harmonically, but the actual chords and their voicing cannot be the same. If you have a bass movement of A-G#-G-F# under an A minor chord with a melody that goes A-B-C-F#, you are plagiarizing (illegally copying) "Stairway to Heaven" and asking to be sued.

In general, when you have finished your song and then play it for friends, pay close attention if anyone says it reminds them of another song. It's a good, safe practice to assume that you may have copied another song inadvertently, so check the words, melody, chords, and accompaniment style to be sure they are different. Even famous writers and bands have been convicted of copyright violation, but they usually have enough money to pay the enormous fines. A book on copyright would be longer than this one, but the issue boils down this: Be as original as you possibly can and don't present the work of others as your own.

KEEP LISTENING

As a songwriter, you never know where ideas will come from. Listen to the people around you and you may be amazed at the stories you hear or the ideas that come to you. The other day I was standing in line at a store when I heard a woman with a distinctive voice tell her male companion that he needed a new hat. Being in a funny mood, and having nothing else to do at the time, my mind wandered and made her words into a short song, which I present here as "Get a New Hat." While it is unlikely to win any awards this season, it shows that ideas can come from anywhere. If I decide to keep the melody, I can either build on the lyrics or write new ones. Here's what I came up with as the people in front of me demanded price checks on almost everything they bought:

Track 1

Of course, I applied some ideas to her simple words. First, I fleshed them out to include "Get a new hat!" Then it struck me that the beginning needed to be repeated. Next I took that section and moved it to a different harmonic area, on a different chord. Since many songs move their main idea down a 5th (or up a 4th), I did that, too. After moving to the G chord I could have progressed back to C, but I wanted to stretch things out a bit, so I dropped back to F then returned to G and came at C via A♭ and B♭. Was this to be a verse or a chorus? We may never know, as I reached the cashier at this point. (We'll take a closer look at this song later in the book.)

Have I mentioned that as a songwriter you may never be bored again? Standing in line or getting stuck in traffic, ideas can come if you are open to them.

SIMPLE OR COMPLEX?

A danger in looking to a favorite artist for inspiration is that we usually give attention to them late in their careers. After all, they become our favorites after we spent years listening to their progression as songwriters and artists. If we try to emulate their later work, we are missing the point of their career: that most artists begin simply and progress in their own direction, into more complex territory. Most songwriters follow this trajectory, only gradually mastering their own style. If you do not master the basics, you will never successfully get beyond them.

You will be much better equipped to judge the value of your songs if you begin simply. Students have come to me with good songs they wanted to reject because "anyone could have written them." Maybe, but the songwriter did write the song, and it is very good! There is the strong possibility for more songs of greater complexity. But for now, you are writing your first song (or even your first after a layoff of some time) and you want it to be good. Listen to one of the most popular songs of the last 50 years, "Hey Jude." Songs don't get much simpler than that, but these simple materials are used to create a song that speaks to millions of people intimately. "Mull of Kintyre" is another.

Some songwriters or songwriting teams (often bands) begin with a set style that may not be immediately popular. Over time, they gather a small group of fans that eventually grows. In this case, the success of the songs is dependent on the success of the band in finding gigs and growing their audience. This is not typical for a songwriter who wants to connect with the audience right away. It is more reminiscent of a group with a cause who are out to spread the word. Since the cause is usually a specific type of music, we will assume you are not in this situation. If you are, then you already know the kind of music you want to write.

In the final analysis, you want to be able to play through your song and be happy with what you have done. It is important to be able to improve early versions of it by finding what you consider to be faults and fixing them. No matter what level of complexity you might start at, the simpler end of the spectrum is easier to work with and leaves you much more room for growth.

SPECIAL NOTE FOR "FAILED" SONGWRITERS

Many readers will have tried to write a song and have what they consider an unfinished mess that is "worthless." This is faulty thinking. You have created ideas for your finished song, and no idea is completely worthless. It is like the home handyman who starts to build a doghouse with no plan and ends up with a lot of lumber nailed into a structure worthy of Picasso that no dog can fit into. While it may need some deconstruction, the materials are still there, and with the right plan a successful doghouse can be achieved. Maybe more wood is needed, or some shingles for a roof, but pieces of what is there are useful.

If you are in this position, take time to review your unfinished songs and pick out parts of any you feel are good or have potential. Let's take an example: You find three rejected songs. One is about your lover leaving you; the second is how good you feel today; and the third is one you gave up on when you realized you were rewriting "Yesterday" in the melody, and yet the words are original. You might combine these scattered bits into an idea that says although your lover left you, you inexplicably feel fine today, and all the woe and heartache belongs to yesterday. Now you have a situation people can relate to, as well as contrasting ideas of sorrow and happiness you can play with in your song. Maybe the verses are sad but the chorus is optimistic; or maybe the verses alternate sad and happy and the chorus comments on how strange life can be. The point is that you can mine your efforts that have been unsuccessful so far and find great songs lurking in there. Think of it as ore: it might be mostly dirt, but you are interested in the gold you know is inside it.

BOTTOM LINE

The songwriting process is slightly different for all of us – and even for each of us at different times in our lives. We are are coming at it from different places with different experiences and differing knowledge, as well as our varying tastes and expectations. Given all of this, it would be amazing if we approached it from the same place. It is also why no single process works for everybody! Our goal here is to find how you write best. And yes, this might include some trial and error, but I'd rather call that fine-tuning because that is really what it is. (For more on this, see Chapter 9: A Sample Song Development.)

Most people will want to begin with part of either a lyric or a melody. If you are completely stumped, this is a good way to start. Once you have part of a lyric you like, set it to a melody; if you get a bit of melody first, try some words. Neither of these has to be the final product, but it is a start. If you have some knowledge of chords, try not to let this interfere with your writing at this stage. Do not get bogged down in choosing the exact right chord yet. You are looking for an idea you like. It won't be finished because it will be an idea you want to work at, but it should be something you like. Once you have a shape to work with, see if you can extend it a bit. At this point, it may be just 20 seconds of music, but if you really like it, that's a great start.

Some people begin with a chord progression, which is OK too. As soon as you have it, try singing over the top of it. The danger here is that you will either sing the top note of each chord, or the bass notes. This can happen unconsciously, and you only recognize that you don't like what you're doing. If you start with a chord progression, consciously search for notes that are in each chord, but don't follow either of the outer notes. This will start out mechanically, but the result will soon be a much smoother song when you join these notes in a flowing line. A good rule of thumb is that if the bass goes down, have your melody go up or stay on the same note. This establishes independence in your melody and also creates a nice sound with the bass of the chords.

You are looking for a starting point. You may end up with a bit of melody you like to the words "My dog Fred" or "My gal Filbertina," but even that should give you an idea of where you are going. What do you want to say about Fred or Filbertina that is special and that others will want to hear about? What cries out to be set to music? How does this beginning continue?

WRITE A SONG!

Use any of the approaches mentioned above to create an idea for a song, or use one that you already have. Take some time to do this. Pick an idea you like and are willing to work at for weeks or even months. It does not have to be your favorite idea (which you might want to save for when you have more experience), but it can be a first shot at it, remembering that you can always write another version. Otherwise, it should be one you like, and will put real energy into finishing. You want to be able to identify two things about the song you create from this idea: when it is finished, and that it is a good song.

Here's the real-life example I mentioned earlier. I'll explain a bit more of my process. Standing in line in a clothing store, a woman behind me asks her male companion: "Why don't you get a new hat?" Something in her voice catches my attention and suddenly my mind is setting her question in a sort of swing rhythm, like this (I'll explain swing in the Rhythm chapter):

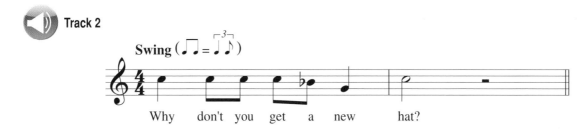

Since my mind does not have a lot else to do while standing there, I come up with an extension to this idea a few seconds before she says the same words:

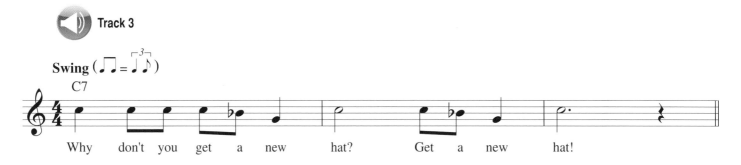

I thought of the idea as starting on C, and recognized that it suggested C7 as the underlying chord. This may not necessarily happen, but if you have a chord in mind with your idea, keep it at least temporarily.

This little snippet is all I mean by "getting started." It is an idea I can work with, one that can grow into something larger. The fact that it came to me so easily outweighed my recognition that the words were silly, but then not every song needs to plumb the depths of the human psyche. The rhythm seems to confirm the lighthearted nature of the words, and it works well with the melody. As I said earlier, I worked on it more while waiting in line, and came up with a longer idea, but even this little snippet would have been a great gift. I could imagine taking it in all sorts of directions: e.g., as Big Band-style swing; as a neo-punk rocker; or even as an ironic sweet ballad. The fact that it is so short leaves all these possibilities open, and imagining them can be real fun.

Walking into the store, I had nothing. Walking out, I had the germ of a new song that I was getting to like and a new pair of jeans – and I only had to pay for the jeans.

CHAPTER 2

WHAT IS A SONG?

Before we even start to think about songwriting, we have to decide what we mean by a song. This is not as simple as it may appear. It might seem so obvious to you that it's hardly worth discussing, no doubt as it seemed to the medieval troubadours and Bach and Beethoven and W.C. Handy and Duke Ellington and George Gershwin and John Lennon. Yet all these writers had completely different ideas of what was so "obvious." Gershwin's songs were sold as sheet music, Lennon's as recordings, and Ellington's are hard to separate from his superb arrangements. Generally speaking, every version of Gershwin's "I Got Rhythm" is equally valid while any version of "Strawberry Fields Forever" is compared to the original recording by the Beatles – considered *the* "correct," authentic version of the song.

For the purpose of songwriting, we will consider a song to be made up of three components: 1) lyrics, 2) melody, and 3) harmony. Each of these can be broken into their constituent parts, but they are clearly separate and essential. The one exception is a purely instrumental "song," which consists only of melody and harmony. We touch on this topic because the issues arising from melody and harmony are the same as in a song with lyrics; in this case, we are writing what Mendelssohn termed "songs without words."

At this point, you may be thinking this is too simple. Just looking at our example of "Strawberry Fields Forever," there is the amazing orchestration, the exotic instruments, the backwards sounds, speeding up and slowing down of parts, not to mention the haunting introduction that identifies the song with just one chord. What about all this?

This is arrangement, the arrangement of a song. A song may have a simple arrangement or a complex one, but it is still a song; even the same song may have vastly different arrangements, but it is still recognizable. Despite different singers, tempo, instruments, groove, improvisations, and studio effects, "the song remains the same" (to quote Led Zeppelin). The core lyrics and melody are unchanged, although the harmony might be different.

The song you write with the assistance of this book will have a simple accompaniment: If you are a guitarist, we will use strummed chords; pianists will use simple repeated chords in the left hand, either with some bass-chord figure or simple arpeggiation. Later, if you decide to create a more complicated arrangement, you will have a solid song to arrange.

Your completed song will be in one of two forms or, even better, in both: a lead sheet or a demo recording. If you can notate your song on manuscript paper or in a computer program, your lead sheet will contain the melody, words, and chord names above the staff (usually in the treble clef). Your demo recording should be a sung version of the entire song with the simple accompaniment. The quality of your voice is not important since the purpose of the demo is to present the song itself; you need not be a great singer, but you must be an *accurate* one. From the recording alone a listener must know that you are singing B and not C, for example.

Thanks to the *Anthology*, we can hear John Lennon's demo recording of "Strawberry Fields Forever," which demonstrates what a great song it is without its mind-blowing arrangement. The reverse is not the case. A poor song cannot be rescued by an amazing arrangement to any but the most superficial listeners. A lot of dance music is like that, where the arranger uses the song as one of the less important layers dominated by the rhythm section – many songs are interchangeable in this style, and the test of a song's real worth is how well it sounds when extracted from its arrangement and played with a simple backing. Many disappear into a repeating formula over a single chord. This is a desirable feature in much dance music, but not the sort of "song" we are aiming to write.

Apply this same test to your favorite songs. Separating the song from its arrangement will teach you more than taking several courses in songwriting. Listen to this music example.

 Track 4

Despite the overblown accompaniment, can you hear the melody in the violins? Try until you can, then verify it with the next example.

 Track 5

MUSIC'S USES

People use music in different ways. Knowing this can be helpful when generating ideas or refining a song. We listen to a lot of music while driving, often to get us energetic (say, on the way to work) or relax us (coming back home). This is a private experience, and people generally are more open to feelings that might be less acceptable in public, such as vulnerability, sadness over loss, or even spiritual striving. If you can envision the situations in which people listen to your music, you will be more successful in connecting with them.

Television and movies provide music to tell the audience how they should feel during certain scenes. In many shows, particularly dramas, this has become the ending song, where a main character's feelings or the overall mood is expressed. This is a specialized and lucrative type of songwriting that takes advantage of music's ability to arouse strong emotion, especially in conjunction with a dramatic situation. It is also one of the few times that music is allowed to step out of the background and onto center stage.

CHAPTER 3

LYRICS

INTRODUCTION

In this chapter, we'll look at lyrics and see what makes them different from poetry. Then we'll consider some of the most popular topics for songs. We will derive some good ideas from the mass of popular songs and see how to apply them to your song while maintaining or defining your style. We'll also examine the perspective you write from, a sometimes overlooked but important aspect of writing.

Every songwriter should try penning lyrics. Unless you want to compose only instrumentals, you will need to know how well you can create words. Besides, it is far too early in your writing career to even know that you want to write only instrumentals. Lyrics are arguably the most important part of a song to your listener since they are the part they understand best; the words will often dictate the direction of your melody. Of course there have been great songwriters who teamed up with a lyricist (from George Gershwin setting his brother Ira's words to Geddy Lee and Alex Lifeson setting the lyrics of Neil Peart), but even here they began writing lyrics as well. In fact, it may be that only after writing your own lyrics, you will be better able to recognize a brilliant lyricist if one should come along.

LYRICS ARE NOT POETRY

For many people, lyrics are the most difficult part of songwriting. "I'm no poet" is a constant refrain, to which the answer is: "Good!" *Lyrics are not poetry.* Poetry may or (increasingly) may not rhyme; lyrics almost always do. Poetry has layers of meaning that take several readings to uncover; lyrics should tell their story the first time a person hears them. Poetry is often intensely personal; lyrics are about our shared experiences, situations that are recognizable to most others. Many people begin to write poetry in adolescence, and when they try to write songs they sometimes attempt to set their poetry to music. This can be difficult for all the reasons just mentioned, especially their personal nature.

Lyrics are frequently confused with poetry because their forms can be similar. There are songs that tell a story like ballad poetry, with verse after verse without the interruption of even a chorus. These might be centuries-old folk songs with a new twist, such as Simon and Garfunkel's "Scarborough Fair/ Canticle." On the other hand, ballads can be newly written, like as Gordon Lightfoot's "Wreck of the Edmund Fitzgerald."

SONG TOPICS

You can write a song about pretty much anything, although so much choice might be a problem in itself. It is worth taking a look at some of the most common topics successful songwriters have chosen. Before we even start, *consider your audience* and think of these categories from *their* point of view. This may be obvious, but you must do it. A "simple love song" will take a different form for a neo-punk audience or an adult contemporary one, while important topics will vary widely depending on the intended listeners. Your time is well spent deciding on who your ideal audience is and writing to them, whether they exist or not. If they do, your music will find them and vice versa. Your only guarantee of failure is to try to please everyone.

Love Songs

Love songs have been the most popular type for as long as people have written songs. From the typical romantic "me and you" lyric to anything that a person can love – these have been the subject of a raft of songs. The world seems never to tire of even the most clichéd versions. Because love is such a universal emotion, love lyrics are best kept somewhat general. A song written to Griselda might thrill all the Griseldas in the world, but it would not be as meaningful to anyone else. "You," on the other hand, can apply to anyone. The other challenge is finding rhymes that have not been so overused that they add an air of unintended comedy to the lyrics: love/dove, moon/June, maybe/baby, and on and on.

Variants of love songs are as varied as life itself. There are songs about breakups, reunions, long-time love, short affairs, "what if," "ships passing in the night," and even egotistical self-love. While irony is difficult to pull off in a popular song, 10cc's "I'm Not in Love" is a great example: The singer desperately tries to convince a person with whom he is madly in love that he is, in fact, not in love.

Story Songs

Telling a story is a great method for generating lyrics. Old-style ballads or epics that consist of a string of verses are interesting chiefly for the tale they tell. Modern story songs can include a chorus that comments on the story, and whose meaning may change as the story unfolds. Paul Simon's adaptation of the poem "Richard Cory" by E. A. Robinson is a good example. The verses narrate Mr. Cory's seemingly ideal life from the viewpoint of one of his factory workers who envies him. The actual emptiness of Mr. Cory's life is revealed in the last line of the final verse, when he commits suicide. In the song, there is a final chorus (unchanged) that shows that, even with this knowledge, the worker would still rather be Cory. While the poem has a powerful effect when this rich, ostensibly carefree man commits suicide, the song has a second one that sinks in more slowly – the depth of misery and envy that blinds the narrator from his false impression of Cory's life.

Humor or Parody

Humor can be surprisingly difficult to convey in songs. The most successful humorous lyrics tend to be broad and obvious. Audience reaction is a good test of humor in a song, but don't try this until you have a certain tolerance for rejection. Novelty songs are often based on observations about life, similar to sketches by stand-up comedians. They may also be based on current fads, so they date rather quickly. Parody is more difficult because you usually have to get permission of the copyright holder to use the music while you create a funny version of the lyrics. Many songwriters begin by parodying songs, and it is great fun, but the decision to include such songs in your performances or recordings is a serious one that requires permissions, which can be difficult to acquire. "Weird Al" Yankovic is the most famous parody artist of the past few decades. Gaining Michael Jackson's permission to parody his songs was undoubtedly his greatest achievement. (You might notice that his parodies are quite mild, and do not make a fool of the original artist.)

Topical Songs

More serious writers are often drawn to a current issue that is important to them, one which they believe others should find crucial as well. Issues change over time, and such songs tend to become dated as the issue subsides or the language used to express it changes. It is also possible to become strident in defense of your position so that you turn off much of your audience, preaching at them. However, a well-written, reasonable, and positive protest song – "We Shall Overcome," for example – can become an anthem for a movement that accomplishes social change. A strong sentiment like this can be applied to any situation involving injustice. This song in particular has been used in a variety of causes with powerful effect. Again, the musical value is important, not just the issue.

Commemorative Songs

Many lyrics commemorate persons, places, and events, ranging from well-known ("Woodstock," "Abraham, Martin and John") to personal ("Our House"). While "Our House" (recorded by CSN&Y) might seem to be overly personal, it celebrates the hippie lifestyle of the times while incorporating elements of a love song. Its lyrics are worth studying for their easy combination of detail ("two cats in the yard") with universal themes ("life used to be so hard"). Finally, the easy-going ambience of the entire production enables the lyricist to use one simple syllable – "la" – for an entire verse without it seeming out of place. Rather than sounding as if words failed the lyricist (which they may have), it adds to the easy, stress-free life pictured by the song.

Most of us want to commemorate someone or something that is meaningful to us. We have to make sure the song resonates with our audience as well, even if they hear it in a way that's different than what we intended. For example, David Gates' "Everything I Own" says he would give just that – everything he owns – to have a particular person back again. Most people assumed it was a love song, and were surprised to learn that he wrote it about his late father. The listener does not need to know the personal story to get the feeling of the song. Most often they apply it to a personal situation anyway, whatever the songwriter may have meant.

Inspirational Songs

Similar to the commemorative genre, inspirational songs include spiritual and religious lyrics, as well as the "you can do it" type. People want to be inspired, but the writer has to find new ways to communicate a timeless message. As with novelty and topical songs, be careful not to include current slang, which may become incomprehensible a few months later, or clichés that sound trite no matter how well-meant.

"If I can do it, anybody can" is one type of song that never seems to get old. It gives people the feeling that they have a shot after all. It can even be inspiring to songwriters! People habitually root for the underdog, even after they have "made it."

Advertising

Many songs are obvious self-advertising for the singer or band performing. Sometimes it is a persona, as in Michael Jackson's "I'm Bad." They can even be humorous, as Ringo Starr singing "I'm the Greatest," written for him by John Lennon, with his tongue planted firmly in his cheek. Some thinly disguise their self-promotion, like Thin Lizzy's "The Boys are Back in Town," while others don't bother. Still others advertise a style of music, "our gang," anything that sets a group apart, or something that brings us all together (leaking into the inspirational genre).

Jingles are the most common type of advertising. The ability to write a catchy, memorable short tune that will stick in the memory (sometimes for decades) is a highly specialized, highly lucrative type of songwriting that is as much psychology and sociology as music. Think of how many of these "ear worms" are crawling around in your brain, some even from your childhood, and you will realize their value to anyone hawking a product. Melody is the crucial ingredient here, specifically the ability to write a new eight-bar phrase that sounds "familiar" on first hearing and that practically anyone will remember. Some advertising agencies keep melody writers on staff, and some have separate lyricists and melodists. There are few people working at the top of this field – and it is not the route for those hoping for fame outside the industry, but it can be the road to riches for those with the knack.

EMOTIONS

Nearly any human emotion is fair game for lyrics, because the emotion will resonate with the listener: hopes, fears, dreams, failures, successes, and the accompanying happiness, anger, or sadness. We all have them and they change over time. If you feel an emotion strongly, you can be sure that there is an audience who feels the same way. Some songs give advice to another person in a difficult situation, showing compassion for the other's emotion. This is exemplified well by "Hey Jude," which has been a comfort to many people in distress; though some of the words may be a bit mystifying, the idea still comes across. Here's a good way to get ideas: Imagine a character (not yourself) who is in a situation that you are not in, but can envision vividly. It could be as simple as a member of the opposite sex getting dumped, or dumping their partner. If you can start to look at life from another's perspective, you will have an endless store of ideas.

PERSPECTIVE

Whether you are writing a love song or narrating a long involved story, it is important to know who is speaking, and to whom. Many writers only write as if they are doing the talking and the listener is assumed to be a close friend. A change of perspective can free up your imagination and make your lyrics more interesting. This can be as simple as changing the subject from yourself to someone else. The Beatles did this effectively when, after writing hit after hit with the basic "I love you" theme, they changed the perspective slightly to "She loves you" and created one of the biggest-selling records of all time. While it was not only the shift of perspective that made the song so irresistible, it helped. There are many variations on this idea: "I love her" (i.e., not you), "She loves him" (i.e., not me), "She loves him" (i.e., not you) and so on.

"I" is called the "first person" in grammar. Writing in the first person means you are telling us about your thoughts and feelings. John Lennon once said he wrote about himself because that was what he knew. The problem here is that it is too easy to be seen as narcissistic if everything is about you.

The "second person" is "you." Writing from this perspective can be tricky because you are either telling the person about themselves or giving advice. Sometimes it can be used like the impersonal "they," as in "You are lucky to see flowers this early in the spring." However, writing about "you" can be a great exercise, perhaps praising someone, or noticing something unique about them. Once more, "Hey Jude" is a first-rate example of using the second person, where Lennon and McCartney use not only the pronoun "you" but Jude's name as well.

The third person – he, she, it, or they – is often used in ballads about particular people, places, or events. Paul McCartney is particularly adept at this, as in his song "Another Day." While writing about yourself in the third person is often creepy ("He sits on the stage staring at you."), it can signal a reflective state of mind where you are outside your regular thought routines and seeing yourself differently: "He looks at the hand he's seen all his life as if it were newly made and wonders at the shapes of the chords it can form, as if without his conscious assistance." You don't have to tell the audience that you are in a pensive mood, because they enter it with you. Another approach is to gradually reveal that "he" or "she" is actually "me." Or maybe you want the song to be creepy, or start as if it is you but then veer off to reveal that it is someone else. There is a lot to explore in any of these "persons."

There are plural versions of each version. "We" or "us" can either include the audience or tell about a separate group of which the singer is a part. "You" in the plural (or "you all" in some regions) speaks to a group outside the singer. "They" is a group that includes neither the singer nor the audience. ("They" is often used to chastise or criticize a practice with the implication "of course *you* wouldn't do this, right?")

Knowing the perspective you are writing from will help you keep from breaking it, such as starting the first verse as "I" and changing it to "he" later (unless this is an effect you want; it's not an easy one to get convincingly). It can also be helpful to realize that you always write from the same perspective, which can be limiting without your knowing why. Conversely, changing person is a great generator of ideas if you get stuck. Try it. Pick a "person" you would not usually write from and try to come up with some ideas from that viewpoint. Even if you don't get a song from it yet, it will open your creative mind to a new experience.

LYRICAL FORMS FOR SONGS

Many songs take their melodic form from that of the lyrics. We have already seen that ballads follow the repeating structure of the words. If lyrics have a section that is repeated between other sections, we usually repeat the music that first went with it, making it a chorus. This suggests that the other parts, if they are about the same length, can be written as verses, and thus use the same melody even though the words change.

Sometimes there are one or two lines that precede the chorus and lead into it from the verse. These often become a "pre-chorus," using the same melody each time, but functioning to build excitement leading into the actual chorus. These may be needed melodically to connect the verse to the chorus, or harmonically to change key or just get to the chord you need. A pre-chorus is separate from the chorus somehow, and may be omitted as a jolt into the final chorus. The pre-chorus does not need to have the same words each time, but it does have to lead to the chorus. A good example of this is "Lucy in the Sky with Diamonds."

Introductions to a song may be instrumental, or they may be implied by the lyrics. This is usually the case if the first "verse" is different from the others, either shorter or longer, maybe providing the setting for the song or some preliminary information necessary to understand what is going on, to set the mood. Lyrical introductions were common in early- to mid-20th century popular songs, and the early Lennon-McCartney song "Bad to Me" imitates this style accurately.

The ending, or "coda" or "outro," is like the introduction but occurs at the end. It may provide a more definitive ending than the chorus, or it may be a necessary "final word" to bring the song to a close. For example, "Yesterday" ends with two bars of humming. Occurring immediately after the words "I believe in yesterday" and using the same melody, the listener hears the words internally and understands that actually singing them would be too obvious. The brilliance of this strategy is that it makes the ending more personal, more internal, while providing a "What more could I say?" ending. Try playing or singing it without the humming!

While these are all basic segments, not all are used or needed in every song. In the final analysis, songs tend to either be ballad-like, repeating the verse over and over; verse and chorus, perhaps augmented with the other sections; or less commonly "through-composed" where little is repeated and it is hard to separate into verses, choruses, or any other form.

Most common is the verse-chorus type of song, where we use the verse to tell the plot of the story, to move the action or emotion along; the chorus underlines the main message or point of the song, tying together the verses. This is usually the best form for a beginner to start with; it must be mastered early in one's songwriting career, in any case. The old Scottish folk song "My Bonnie Lies Over the Ocean" is a classic example of this type. Its first verse is so well known that many people mistake it for a chorus, at least until the real chorus comes in.

The lyrics, as published in 1881, are:

My Bonnie lies over the ocean,
My Bonnie lies over the sea,
My Bonnie lies over the ocean,
Oh, bring back my Bonnie to me.

Chorus
Bring back, bring back,
Bring back my Bonnie to me, to me;
Bring back, bring back,
Bring back my Bonnie to me.

Last night as I lay on my pillow,
Last night as I lay on my bed,
Last night as I lay on my pillow,
I dreamt that my Bonnie was dead.

Oh, blow the winds o'er the ocean,
And blow the winds o'er the sea,
Oh, blow the winds o'er the ocean,
And bring back my Bonnie to me.
Chorus

The winds have blown over the ocean,
The winds have blown over the sea,
The winds have blown over the ocean
And brought back my Bonnie to me.
Chorus

The first verse shows how simple lyrics can be and yet still be effective. If we use letters to indicate lines, we could call the form of the verse's lyrics aa'ab. The first line is slightly modified to create line 2, then line 1 is repeated, and a new idea is presented to end the verse. This same structure is used in each verse.

Repetition is used here pretty much to the extreme of the listener's tolerance, yet the song continues to be recorded in updated settings, admittedly with changes to the lyrics. While the lyrics are no longer the main attraction of the song, they have survived for centuries. Any beginning songwriter should be proud of writing lyrics as good as these.

The verses clearly tell the story: Bonnie is far away and her paramour wishes her to return; he fears that harm may come to her; he asks the winds that carried her away to carry her back; the wind complies and returns her to him. The chorus repeats his prayer for her return. The message is universal: Who cannot relate to a lover being far away – physically or emotionally – and longing for their return? The words can be taken literally or figuratively, with no need for complicated analysis.

Notice how the words work with the melody, so that word accents match musical accents. Try it, both here and with lyrics you write yourself. Speak them first and then sing them; the accent patterns should match. If you find accents that don't match properly, as in "My Bon-NIE lies o-VER the o-CEAN," you have more work to do. But as you have seen, it is work that is possible. This is just one more challenge, *not* an indicator that you "cannot write lyrics."

 Track 6

Like learning to play an instrument, this will take time, practice, and patience with yourself. Most often it is a simple change to the melody, such as a subdivision of note values if you wanted to write "My Barbara Ann lies over the ocean," for example. Of course, there can come a point where a rethink might be necessary, say for "My Barbara Antoinette lies over the ocean…"

Rhyme patterns can be suggested by melodic patterns and vice versa. Remember that you do not have to use rhyming couplets, the pattern aabbccdd, etc. Experiment with different schemes such as abcb, where the odd-numbered lines do not rhyme but the even ones do. This is easier to manage and can sound more natural than forcing every single line to rhyme with another somewhere. Rhyming dictionaries can be helpful, but don't run out to buy just any one. Remember the first time you realized that someone had recently bought a thesaurus because they started using all sorts of fancy words to say the same thing over and over unnecessarily? This is the same sort of effect, where a songwriter does not rhyme "moon" with "June" or "love" with "dove," but instead opts for "ethereal" and "sidereal."

If you find that you cannot come up with convincing rhymes on your own, you might want to buy a good rhyming dictionary, but use it carefully. Find and use words that are natural to you and your audience. Get one that uses multi-syllable words that rhyme, since all rhyming words don't need to have the same number of syllables. Some even include phrases that rhyme with other phrases, or single words. To use one of these books successfully, the final lyrics must sound like something you or your audience would ordinarily write or say.

You do not always need to write as yourself. "Confessional" songs, like confessional poetry, can get pretty tiresome and are likely to become personally embarrassing in the future. Avoid this by shifting a personal situation to something others can share. Instead of "Jill, my raven-haired, hazel-eyed girlfriend of two years and the best late-night bartender in Houston" write about "my beautiful lover" (Whose isn't?) and keep to details that will interest anyone listening. This is not to say avoid all detail, but since you have so few words you can fit into a song, make each one count, and make each detail important to the situation.

Many songwriters begin with the words. This can make writing the melody easier because you will know where the accents fall; they tend to slide into place as your melody takes shape. Keep in mind, though, that the lyrics so far are a draft. Never be afraid to change the words to fit a great melody. Don't commit to either too early, but stay open to better ideas if they arrive.

LISTEN TO YOUR LYRICS

Lyrics are meant to be heard. Sing your lyrics, even on a single note if you don't have your melody yet, to hear how they sound. Once you have a draft of your melody, sing them again and listen for spots that don't sound quite right. You do not need to do a full analysis of every accent in every bar, but you should do that full type of analysis for any spot that sounds wrong to your ear. It is most likely that you are hearing a clash of accents between the meter, rhythm, and words.

Just speaking the words is not nearly as productive, and is liable to discourage you. Many lyrics sound weak on their own, gaining their true strength only when coupled with a melody. Some comedians have routines where they recite lyrics as if they were grand poetry, and of course the lyrics come off sounding foolish. But give these same words a suitable melody, a powerful singer, and a compelling accompaniment and they can be as moving as the finest poetry.

Don't shoot yourself in the foot by expecting more from your lyrics than they are meant to deliver. If they get your point across, express the feeling you intend, and don't sound wrong when sung, they are doing their job. Melody and harmony have to pull their weight, too.

CHAPTER 4
MELODY

The most important element of your song is its melody. The importance of lyrics can vary, but without a good melody you do not have a good song. A good melody can redeem bland words, or even stand on its own as an instrumental; it can use the barest chords as background or survive an over-zealous application of sophisticated chords; it might have a great accompaniment or be sung on its own. Most of our examples will be in major keys; minor has the complication of a leading tone that is not in the key signature. For an in-depth discussion of this, see Chapter 7: Harmony.

The gift for writing melody is, to a large degree, inborn. Some of the great classical composers were not great melodists, but every great songwriter was or is a great writer of melodies. Much of what I can tell you is how to improve a melody once you have written it, and what mistakes to watch out for, but no one can tell you how to write a great melody. There is no formula. I can tell you how to write a *well-formed* melody, but that does not ensure greatness. This is the true challenge of songwriting: that we aim all our lives to write better and better melodies. Songwriting never becomes stale because music has infinite possibilities and we only ever scratch the surface. This, more than any other technical reason, is why you need to finish your first song: so that you have something to improve upon. This is taking the first step on a journey that will last a lifetime, with many fascinating discoveries along the way.

VOCAL VS. INSTRUMENTAL

Many aspiring songwriters begin with instrumentals because they are uncomfortable writing lyrics. The better approach is to consider the characteristics and advantages of both and choose the one that fits your song better. For example, singers need to breath, whereas a pianist's fingers do not.

Many times, you will come across a word phrase that seems like a great lyric to include in a song. This verbal idea often comes with a melody that fits it; it is a good idea to get both of them down quickly and accurately. Over-thinking a melody is a trap you can avoid by keeping your initial idea – as long as you don't come up with something much better. We tend to forget the emotional charge that such an idea gives us when we first think of it, but by keeping as much detail as possible we can regain that feeling later as long as we have enough information – not just the words and pitches, but the tempo, the chords (if we have them in the original idea), the instrument (if appropriate), and even the type of accompaniment if that was part of it. (A few sparse piano notes gives a different feel from strongly strummed guitar chords.) Keep a recording device at hand, even when just "fooling around." If you are feeling in the mood or the zone, leave it recording all the time – you can easily edit out the dead space or bad ideas. It's easier to delete a bad idea than to re-create a terrific one you've forgotten. Become familiar with your recorder before you need it, so you don't lose that great idea while figuring out how to start recording. Know your machine well, so you don't lose your hard-won phrase by accidentally deleting it or recording over it.

Another advantage to continuous recording is that you will see how quickly your mind moves away from the original idea. Many times, I've been about to give up on a song because I thought the idea was going nowhere, but then on moving back in the recording to listen to the original idea, I find I still like it, but have just taken it in a direction I don't like. This procedure can save some great ideas you might otherwise toss away. Beginners are especially susceptible to throwing out good ideas for lack of confidence. Save every idea you like, even if you decide not to work on it right away. You will be glad to have them later when you want to work on a song, but yet don't have a good enough idea. You might even realize that what you thought was a vocal melody works better as an instrumental, or vice versa.

Vocal music has limitations you need to keep in mind. The singer needs to breathe at regular intervals. If the song has lots of notes, especially high or loud ones that require more breath, these breathing spaces need to be more frequent and longer toward the end. Singers can articulate words only so quickly, and English is not the easiest language to sing at a fast tempo. Too many words sung quickly can sound humorous – as in REM's "It's the End of the World as We Know It (And I Feel Fine)" – almost becoming an auctioneer's voice. At the other end of the spectrum, a vocalist can hold a note for only so long, and the maximum length shortens as the note gets louder because it requires more breath. Finally (for now), the range of the melody is important. Singers are used to transposing songs into keys that fit their voices, but even in the best key there is still a limit as to how high and how low the singer can go. Unless you are writing for yourself or another specific individual, you should keep to a modest range. For example, the Beatles often wrote songs with large ranges, but when writing specifically for Ringo they reduced the range considerably, in some cases to only a perfect 5th. (That's quite a challenge; try it some time.)

Instrumental music is not constrained by vocal issues, so wider, faster, more "breathless" melodies are often best used as instrumentals. The limitations usually arise from the instrument itself, which the songwriter needs to keep in mind. For example, a piano note fades away quickly and once struck cannot be made to get louder. This is easy on a violin or synthesizer. Otherwise the limitations on piano are largely due to the expertise of the player. Other instruments have their own special effects, such as note-bending on a guitar, or the different types of slides between notes on the white keys of the piano versus the semi-tonal slide on a guitar string, to the smooth slide through all frequencies on a violin or slide guitar. Sometimes you will need to change instruments to use your idea; at other times, you may change your idea to suit your preferred instrument.

In the final analysis, some melodies must be played instrumentally because they are impossible to sing. Otherwise it is mostly the songwriter's choice. Once the decision is made, the medium can be exploited or not. The more specifically a melody is written for a particular instrument, the less likely it is to work on another; it is restricted to its intended instrument or those of the same instrumental "family." For example, Bach's cello suites work well on a viola because it is tuned just like a cello, but an octave higher. They are also popular on the guitar, where several of the constraints reverse: The arpeggios that cause such dramatic movement of the bow and give a sense of strain to the original are easy on the guitar, while the simple scale passages done with one smooth stroke of the bow are much harder on the guitar. They work because the balance is kept, but in reverse.

If you listen to a lot of music – and as a songwriter you should listen to a *lot* of different music – you will notice that most of it is made up of wavelike patterns that rise to a peak and then fall back from it, over and over, especially the melodies. It is the speed of the rise and descent, along with the heights and depths of the waves, which give each melody its shape or contour. In many ways, this shape will be more important to you than the notes that make it up. The shape can be the basis for variation that still sounds similar to the ear.

SECTIONS AND RESTS

No doubt you have noticed that melody breaks up into sections rather than coming at you in one continuous spew. The more you pay attention, the more of these sections you will find at smaller and smaller levels.

At the largest level, there are individual verses and choruses. Each of these is made up of one or more musical statements. Statements are made up of phrases, and while it is not terribly important for you to know dictionary definitions of each, think of a statement as a series of phrases that ends in a full cadence. A phrase usually ends in a half cadence, or more rarely no cadence, unless it is the last phrase in a statement. This is like the phrases in a sentence: You can have a whole bunch of them, and they are usually separated by commas, but the last one ends with a period.

Let's say you have a lyric like this: "I just can't stop thinking of you, thinking of all the things that you do." We usually don't write lyrics out like this. In fact, we usually write lyrics out so that we can see where the pauses – the rests – are expected. So for our sample lyric, we would more likely write it like this:

> I just can't stop
> Thinking of you,
> Thinking of all
> The things that you do

These are short phrases, but they remind us of what we were thinking as we wrote the lyrics. The comma after the second line seems to say that there is a rest there (maybe a more formal one like a half cadence) and the lack of punctuation after the last line suggests that the idea does not stop there. So the song might end up sounding like this:

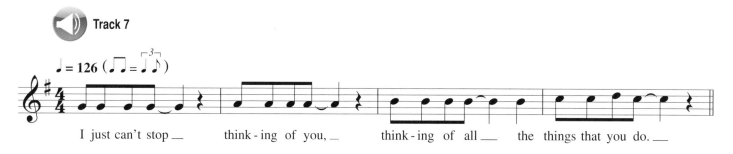

Track 7

Sometimes we think of rests as there just to fill up the leftover space in a bar, but they provide an important function: They separate the phrases clearly. Perhaps you can think of several different melodies that would suit these words, and I suggest you try. As you do, notice how you separate the phrases with rests. Seriously, go ahead before reading on. Try a couple of melodies.

Did you use more rests than the example did, or fewer? Did you hold some notes longer (such as on the word "stop") rather than inserting a rest? No matter how you used rests, you most likely put one where the comma was originally, one that splits the lyric fragment in half. This is a typical place for a cadence.

In this example, I added a tempo or timing mark, saying that the speed is 126 beats per minute (bpm) with the quarter note as the beat unit. (If you don't have a metronome, buy one. Some FX pedals have them built in, as does some software, but if these are not handy or easy to use, buy a dedicated one. Be sure to get a metronome that has "tap tempo" so you can tap your beat and it will tell you the speed.) We will discuss tempo more in Chapter 6 (Rhythm), but you should be thinking about it as you write any melody. (You probably are, even if you don't realize it.) If you take the example above and play it at 192 bpm it will sound comical and ridiculous. The music outruns the thought and the constant stopping sounds out of breath. At the opposite end, slowing it down to 66 bpm makes it sound like a student's scale exercise.

Track 8
192 bpm

Track 9
66 bpm

In each case, we are so far from the natural spoken rhythm that it fails to make much sense. You don't always have to sing at the speed you would speak the words, but keep in mind that changing the speed of speaking creates a certain effect, which is often amplified in singing. Slowing down and speaking more deliberately can communicate caring in a romantic situation, or barely controlled anger in a confrontation. These translate into similar effects in a love song or a protest song. Speeding up in both speech and singing usually translates into excitement. The type of excitement is a product of the words rather than the speed, but the tempo enhances it and should not contradict it.

All the elements work together. The speed works with the sections, which work with the pitch arcs (or waves), which interact with the harmony, all of which express the words. It sounds almost mathematical when we deal with one element at a time, but dealing with them all at once, as a songwriter usually does, is what makes music art rather than science. Hard work and constant experimentation are the keys to success both in music and in science – especially when we learn from our mistakes.

MOTIVES

Let's return to our example of "My Bonnie Lies Over the Ocean" to see how "waves" work.

Track 10

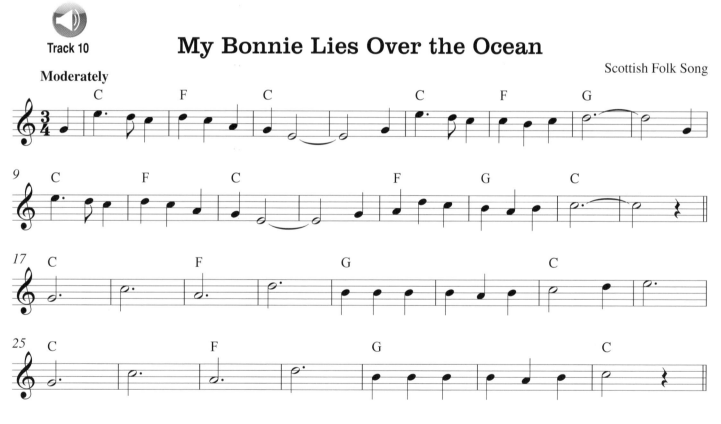

Each melodic wave here is four bars long. The first four bars show a distinctive shape, with a leap from G up to the highest note E. This leap of a major 6th is unusually large. Now look at the first note in each of the next three bars: They fall to D, G, and finally E an octave lower than the high note. Within this overall wave shape are smaller motions, like the move D-C-D from bar 1 to bar 2, and the C and A in bar 2 that break up and slow down the drop to the low E.

The second phrase from bars 5–9 starts off with the same notes, but hangs onto the C from bar 6 so that bar 7 uses the neighbor-note motion from bars 1–2 where it was D-C-D, only now it is C-B-C, which leads up to the high D. Instead of dropping like the previous one, this wave stays up high, while reusing the start of a previous idea.

Phrase 3 is an exact copy of phrase 1, just as the third line of the lyrics is a copy of the first. We now have phrases that 1) went high to low; 2) stayed high; and 3) went high to low. Balance suggests that our last phrase will somehow end up in the middle, which is just what bars 13–16 do: After a gentle rise to D, the line moves by step down to B where the neighbor-note idea is repeated to lead it up to C.

The melody has a sense of wide breadth, even though it spans only an octave. This is due mainly to the large leap at the start of the melody, which is used to start three of the four phrases. A recurring feature such as this is called a motive (or motif). These can be repeated literally, as the G to E move is, or they can be similar, like the leap from A to D in bar 13 where the 6th becomes a 4th and is moved onto beat 1. In fact, this one is so changed we might not even notice it as a motive if it had not been used at the beginning of the phrase.

Another motive is the neighbor note, where a note moves to the next (neighbor) note below or above it, before returning to the original note. Neighbor notes in "My Bonnie" are the D-C-D of bars 1–2, the C-B-C of bar 6 and the B-A-B of bar 14. These motives subtly tie together the melody by using the same moves at different spots. Often you will find that you have put similar motives into your melodies just because they make musical sense. But if you find yourself stuck, wondering what to do at some spot in a melody, it can be helpful to look at motives you have been using; see if one fits your problem spot.

The chorus begins at bar 17, and as with many successful choruses it is simpler than the verse and uses memorable motives from the verse, but in a different way. While the big leap of a 6th is a memorable motive, it has been used a lot in the verse, so it is better to use the variation of it from bar 13, the rising 4th. This is the whole melody of bars 17–20, the rising 4th repeated. Before this gets boring, bar 21 breaks up the dotted-half note into three quarter notes, which then become the neighbor-note motive in bar 22, which resolve to the C in bar 23. The D and E that follow are more important than they may seem. First, they keep the melodic motion going. (Try singing the chorus and leaving them out; it comes to a dead stop without them.) On a more subtle level, this whole eight bars stretches out the original move from G to E, the first two notes of the verse. Whether intended or just happy accidents, it is subtleties like these that have kept this song popular for centuries. The second eight bars of the chorus are identical, except that they leave off the last two notes and so come to a final cadence.

You may be thinking that "My Bonnie Lies Over the Ocean" is too simple, but its lesson is that simple songs can capture the ears and imagination of generations of people and last for centuries. Think of "Greensleeves" or "Scarborough Fair." No one realizes how difficult it can be to write a simple yet convincing song until they try. Even Beethoven worked for ten years to create the simple theme to his "Ode to Joy." He had to continually work at simplifying his complex ideas until the melody seemed so naïve as to be natural.

"Morning Has Broken"

A traditional Scottish melody is the basis of "Morning Has Broken." In fact, the sung melody is just the old hymn tune "Bunessan," while the instrumental surrounding parts were intended for a different song until Cat Stevens convinced Rick Wakeman to use them in his version of the song.

We have seen the unusually repetitive form of the song, which is saved from monotony by a skillful melody. Looking at it in 9/4 keeps each motive together in one bar, so let's use that version. The three quarter notes followed by two dotted-half notes is a rhythmic motive that is varied. Notice how many of the three quarter-note segments are based on the tonic triad, C major. Bar 1 arpeggiates it upward, while bars 4 and 6 go downward. Bar 3 adds a passing note on D so that the first dotted-half note is now part of the upward arpeggiation; this same idea works in bar 5 so that the "missing" C at the start is the high note now. The linking of E-G with the C major triad carries the idea to bar 7, and bar 8 reverses the order of E-D-E to D-E-D to lead to the cadence.

"Yesterday"

As stated previously, melody moves in waves, both large and small. Consider "Yesterday." It starts with just two notes, the second one repeated. After the first word, it arcs up to the high point of the melody on "so far," and from there it descends in a series of waves that slowly falls back to the starting notes. This is not a random design, or even a standard pattern; it follows the sense of the words. At first there is a memory of the past without the current problems, and the song soars upward. But gradually the realization of the current problems and how they are not going away soon pulls down the high spirits as depressing thoughts do. Notice how, after the one big rise, there are several smaller "wavelets" that fall, making the descent more gradual. At the end of the first verse, the beginning word is repeated – but rising, instead of falling. This is a master touch that serves two purposes: it is a subtle reminder of how much better yesterday was; it sets up verse two, so that it can start with the same motion down as verse one.

Motives are used subtly here, too. The first three notes that give the title also provide a simple, memorable motive. McCartney changes it slightly each time: drawing out the first note a bit on "far away"; drawing it out even longer on "here to stay"; and then using this same rhythm, but going up a major 3rd instead of down, to end the verse on "yesterday." If you sing both these versions of the word "yesterday," their melodies don't seem too related. But by gradually changing the rhythm of the three notes every two bars, we come to expect a version of the motive, and one that is slightly different. (Sing all four and you will hear the connection.)

"Yesterday" is such a familiar song, and its verse so well crafted, that many people overlook its somewhat strange structure. It is the verse that is memorable, and that contains the title. In fact, there is no chorus, just a "middle eight" – eight bars of contrast that pick up the melodic A at the end of the verse, leaping up from it to a high note of F, the same high note of the verse. Even the chords used are virtually identical to the verse. What makes it such a strong song? An exceptional melody.

ANTECEDENT-CONSEQUENT

Most melodies are made up of two parts: an antecedent (first) phrase (usually four bars) and a consequent (end) of the same length. The antecedent sets up an expectation, and the consequent continues on, usually fulfilling the expectation. From the harmonic point of view, the antecedent often ends on a half cadence, while the consequent finishes with a full cadence. The melodic arcs or waves reinforce the division of the melody as well as the climax point (highest or most accented note).

"Amazing Grace" is a clear example of an antecedent phrase of seven bars (the last note of which is indicated by the arrow) followed by a consequent phrase of seven bars as well. The antecedent phrase has two broad arcs, one leading up to the B in bar 1, which then falls back to the starting D, and a second that leads up to the melodic climax on the high D at the end of the antecedent phrase in bar 7. (We don't count the single-note upbeat bar at the start as a bar when numbering.) While the length of the sections is not typical, this example shows that, even in such cases, the antecedent-consequent structure works seamlessly.

Track 12

Amazing Grace

Traditional American Melody

Moderately

Here, the consequent sounds right because it is so similar to the antecedent. It is the same length, and even has the same midpoint descent to the low D. The half cadence of the antecedent is answered by the full cadence of the consequent, which the melody stresses even more by ending the antecedent on the dominant note and the consequent on the tonic. The last phrase is approached by a wave from D up to B, as at the start, but now it falls back to the tonic G.

Much of the antecedent's music is reused by the consequent. Aside from the cadence, most differences are due to accommodating the lyrics. Look at the phrase from the start to bar 4; the next phrase from bars 4–7 is almost the same, except for the shortened ending. Bars 7–11 are different, while bars 11–14 are another shortened version of the first phrase. We can use letters to signify phrases, and so call this an AABA form. Notice that each A is slightly different from the others. Some books would label this AA'BA" but that notation is a bit picky for us. Just remember that any repeated section (e.g., A) may be slightly varied.

SONG FORMS

Songs are written in different forms, many of which are standardized. Melodically, harmonically, and rhythmically they are made of up sections that are either repeated – exactly or with slight variations – or that are contrasting. Once again, the ideas of repetition of the familiar and the introduction of new material are at work to keep the song coherent and interesting.

You are most likely familiar with songs that have verses and choruses. A verse is a repeated section whose words change each time through, while a chorus keeps the same words each time and is often the high point of the song. This is such a common and useful format that I suggest you use it for your first few songs to gain mastery of this most important form. As meaningful as lyrics can be, most forms are based on the structure of the melody. We use letters to designate sections that are the same or similar, just as we did with phrases earlier. The context tells us what units the letters represent.

As we have seen, verse-chorus songs may have optional elements, such as an introduction (or intro) or coda (ending or outro). These are added on at either end, to lead into the song in a specific way or to make the ending more final or effective. Sometimes sections are added in the middle of a verse-chorus arrangement as well. An instrumental can give the singer a break and a soloist a chance to shine; these are usually played over the chords of the verse, more rarely over the chorus. Some songs have a pre-chorus that is added to build up more excitement from the verse to lead into the chorus. This is a slightly advanced technique that you do not need for a successful first song, although if by instinct you put one into your song you should know it for what it is, especially since a poorly written pre-chorus can reduce the impact of a good chorus.

Verses and choruses are customarily written as eight- or 16-bar units, most often divided into four-bar phrases. This is not an iron-clad rule, but merely the most commonly used formula. Same-sized units make up larger units; this symmetry has an appeal in all types of music. Because of this, deliberately created asymmetrical phrases can be quite powerful

The 32-bar (or AABA) form is also commonly used in pop songs, many of which have become jazz standards. As its two names imply, this form is comprised of two different parts, A and B, each of which is eight bars long. This simple form contains only 16 bars of different music, since A is repeated three times, although its melody is usually changed slightly to accommodate differing words. In reality, most of these "standards" are the choruses of the original song. The lack of variation is made up for by improvisations that differ with each repetition, as a different instrument "takes a chorus."

"Yesterday" is an interesting example of how all this works together in a song that is considered both a pop song and a standard. It both follows the "rules" and breaks them, and yet sounds flawless. "Yesterday" cannot be considered a 32-bar form because the A section is seven bars long, while the B section is eight bars. The song consists of a two-bar introduction, then AABABA with a two-bar coda (or outro). After the original AABA form, the song is extended with another BA. This song does not divide neatly into verse and chorus, so it is most easily described by letters. The first section (A) is repeated, then the B is introduced for variety, and A returns to round it off. At this point, because we have heard A three times already, B returns before another A ends the song, rounded off by a two-bar coda that matches the two-bar intro.

Notice the simplicity of the guitar accompaniment on this classic song. While the strings add an extra dimension, the song is superb with simple strumming. Listen to just the first three bars, and then imagine beginning the song without the intro, starting immediately with the word "yesterday." It is abrupt and changes the introspective mood of the song. What a powerful change is made with the simplest of accompaniment figures. The coda is similarly compelling – short but absolutely necessary, while humming rather than singing is inspiration at its finest. What words could possibly add to that which has already been said?

This song can teach us so much. Trust your ear more than rules or advice. If a section works as seven bars, don't try to drag it out to eight. Likewise, if it works as nine, don't try to cut it back to eight. A good song will stand on its own with the simplest accompaniment; don't be afraid to keep it basic. Pay extra attention to the intro because it sets the mood and is your listener's first impression of the song, even after repeated hearings. Similarly, take additional care with the coda since it is your "last word" and the listener's final impression of the song.

This last point is worth emphasizing. For your first few songs at least, you should plan a strong, definite ending rather than a fade-out. While fades are popular on recordings, they are not as effective in live performance, and should never be used to disguise an inability to end a song definitely.

The AAB form of the blues, typically 12 bars long, is a variation of the AABA form. Do not begin by writing the blues unless you are an experienced blues player committed to the genre. Excellence in the blues is subtle; it is easy to write mediocre blues song that inadvertently sounds like satire. As we noted earlier, humor is hard to write in music; you want your audience to laugh *with* you, not *at* you. And if only from the standpoint of craft, this form will not allow you to expand into other areas as you need to. Think of it this way: Because of its restricted breadth of form, the blues demands early on that you develop depth and commitment that is beyond most beginners, regardless of age or other musical experience.

Many other musical forms follow the lyrics, essentially setting words to melodies that follow the words' form. Ballads are the classic example, where a series of verses is guided by a set pattern that reflects the rhyme scheme. Lowercase letters are used to represent the sound of the words at the end of a line; the same letters indicate that the words rhyme. So a lyric that follows the rhyme scheme abcb will most often use the same music for the 'b' lines (that rhyme), and usually (but not always) similar music for "a" and "c" as well:

Lyrics: abcb
Melody: ABAB or AABA (or ABCB)

The variations on this idea are endless, as are the variations in rhythm scheme in verse. It is important to remember that lyrics are not poetry, so we are talking about rhyme schemes as a lyric device, not a poetical one. Rhymes have a pleasing sound and make the lyrics easier for the singer to remember. They are also a guide for the songwriter in determining the melodic structure, or – if the structure or melody came first – a method of strengthening the effect.

A ballad can be comprised simply of a succession of verses. This puts the emphasis on the lyrics, which usually tell a compelling story. A ballad requires a melody that can accommodate a variety of situations; we want one that doesn't emphasize any single action or emotion too strongly, a melody that is objective yet interesting.

A ballad may contain a chorus, which can restate the general theme of the song. Again, this emphasizes the lyrics. A clever use of a chorus (or refrain) in a ballad is one in which the changing words take on a different significance as the situation changes in the verses, sometimes going so far as to mean its opposite by the end of the song. Paul Simon's "Richard Cory" does exactly that.

To summarize: There are many different song forms, but it's best to start with verse-chorus. As a songwriter you *must* master this form, and the earlier the better. Song forms are a lifelong fascination for songwriters, and as with any art or craft, the best basis is a mastery of the most important elements. All of these can be found in the verse-chorus form.

Repetition of the First Section (AAAB and AAB)

Some melodies repeat a short phrase, often with small adjustments to fit into the harmony, changing only for the last phrase so that the song is brought to a convincing end (AAAB). This is similar to the AABA form we have seen, but the A must bear repetition three times, while the B needs to provide a convincing ending. The chorus to "The Blue Tail Fly" (aka "Jimmy Crack Corn") is a classic example: The title phrase is repeated three times and a new phrase is introduced to end the melody convincingly. The repetitions build up an expectation of something new, and each one increases the tension. This would be a dangerous place to frustrate the listener's expectation, and a fourth repetition would just make the song boring.

The repetitions may sound the same to a casual listener, but they are modified slightly to fit the harmony. Bar 3 moves the Fs to G (and the final E) to fit into the C chord. This moving upward continues in bar 4 where the Gs after beat 1 one go up to A. On the third repetition, the words "I don't care" continue the upward motion to the B♭ and then leap up to the high point of the melody – the note D – before the new phrase ends the melody with the full cadence C7–F.

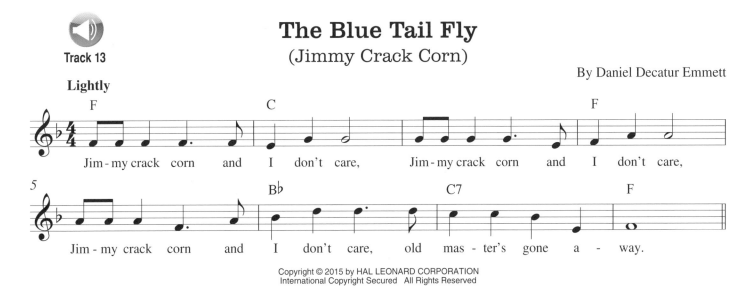

The Blue Tail Fly
(Jimmy Crack Corn)

By Daniel Decatur Emmett

The repetition of a short phrase of lyric changes the melody to fit the harmony, and also subtly leads to the climax of bar 6. It is different from the antecedent-consequent type of melody, in one way by having a full cadence at the end of each four-bar segment. This would sound boring if our ears were listening for an eight-bar melody built from two four-bar phrases, but the repeated lyric tells us that something else is going on. The melody is crafted so that it rises by step on every repetition, fitting only the tonic and dominant chords until it reaches a climax on the subdominant B♭. The final phrase differs; it flows down from the high point and ends strongly, outlining a V7–I cadence with the leading tone going to the tonic in the melody.

The blues' AAB form is similar with its repeated four-bar first phrase, but then the melody ends with a different third four-bar phrase, which provides its characteristic 12-bar structure. Since blues also has a characteristic harmonic structure, the types of cadence are dictated by the blues patterns themselves. This means that the two A sections will differ, but only to fit the chord pattern. The simplest example is that the first A might be harmonized entirely with the tonic chord (expressed in blues as a dominant 7th sonority, so a blues in C would have a C7 tonic). The next A would have to fit over a IV7 chord for its first two bars, and then back to the tonic for the next two. Because there are common notes between the I7 and IV7 chords (if we count the "blue" 3rd) it is possible for the melody to stay the same, or it may differ. In either case, the final B section rounds off the form and ends it back on the tonic. If more verses are required, the final chord can be V7 to start it all over again. There is no split into verse and chorus because there is only one 12-bar section of music.

Standard Form (AABA)

AABA is the form of many songs that are considered "standards," especially by jazz players. It is also considered standard by many songwriters who default to its form when writing. As we saw in "The Blue Tail Fly," the AAAB form tends to use small sections; in that example, each section was just two bars long. This helps to keep the triple repetition from becoming boring. The blues' AAB form uses four-bar sections to give it its overall 12-bar length. Four bars are adequate for a slow tempo such as modern blues has. Older blues were played faster, and sometimes the sections were eight bars, still maintaining the relationship between them. In AABA form, both A and B are usually eight-bar sections. We have seen that other lengths are possible, as in the seven-bar A section of "Yesterday," but eight bars is the norm for each.

The A section in AABA is often varied because it has so many roles to play. First, it must have a strong beginning to get the listener's interest right away. It must be capable of being repeated immediately. If the chords change on this repeat, it must be recognizable as the same basic structure, adapted to the underlying chords or to the lyrics. The B section provides contrast, but in this form it does not end the song; it leads back into the A section. The final A section has to provide a convincing ending as much as it provided a strong start. This is done quite often by altering the ending to fit a strong cadence.

Because AABA is only 32 bars long (and is sometimes called 32-bar form), it is often stretched out to make a longer song (although the 32-bar chorus is a favorite for jazz players to improvise over). Again, "Yesterday" is a great example, because it adds an extra BA to make the form AABABA, as well as an intro and a coda.

...AND MORE

There are more sections that can be added to songs. The AABA or any other form can be a verse and/or a chorus. A completely new idea can be introduced as a bridge or instrumental break or, as we saw earlier, a pre-chorus. You are not tied to a pre-set formula for writing your song, but they should give you ideas and guidance when you are stuck. If your song is too repetitive, it's a good bet you have too many A sections and not enough contrasting Bs. Similarly, if you write a song that fits any of these formulas and it is too short, you will either need to repeat part or come up with a new idea that fits what you have so far. Maybe AABA BA CBA (where C is whatever you want)? In the early 1980s, the band Genesis wrote the song "ABACAB," where the title was a description of the song's form.

TYPICAL MELODIC MISTAKES & HOW TO AVOID THEM

Can't leave home

Many attempts at melody continuously circle and return to the same note. You may not hear this because you are so close to your work, but your listeners will. The song becomes annoying and boring. To avoid this, pay special attention to the notes that each of your phrases begins and ends on. Then look at the movement of melodic waves. The same note can sound varied over different chords, so looking at a score can be helpful.

Hyperactivity

The opposite extreme is a melody made up of leaps that display vocal agility, but seem to have no plan or structure. This is a less common problem, one you can avoid by balancing the number of skips with the number of scalar passages in your melody. There is no mathematical formula to say how much of each is too much, so listen to lots of melodies and take your cue from those you really like. Remember that the wavelike motion is usually made up of small steps with an occasional jump. However, lots of leaps sometimes gives a feeling of strength and confidence, as in "My Bonnie Lies Over the Ocean," which is a highly organized song.

Save a note; don't spend them all at once

Even with seven notes in a scale, things can get boring if you fire off all of them at once. It can be striking to save a note for the second half of your melody, or for the high point, or even for the chorus. Our ears naturally react to a note that has not been heard before, and it draws our attention. This can often save a melody that is "almost there," but is a bit dull as is. For example, "Amazing Grace" saves the high D (in G major) for its climax.

Less may be more, or better

Songs often become more complex as you continue to work on them. This can happen so slowly that you don't realize you have over-burdened your melody with too many notes or chords. If you feel bogged down with your melody, sing it over and listen for spots that sound too busy or just different from the rest. It is easier to add than to take away notes, but sometimes they have to be cut. At times, you even have to sacrifice phrases that you really like for the sake of the song as a whole. Save these for later songs. A word of advice, though: If your melody gets better and better as it gets busier and busier, but harder to sing, you may have an instrumental on your hands.

Start with an X-ray

Sometimes you will run into several problems at once, and feel like throwing in the towel. If this happens, lay out the skeleton of your melody. This is an organizational technique that can be used to start a melody, but it's also useful to salvage one. This is particularly handy if you have the words already, or a strong sense of where your melody will be headed. Plan out the notes you want to cadence on, the last notes in each phrase. Add the high note of your melody if you have a good idea of where you would like it.

In the example on page 36, I sketch out a skeletal idea: start on G, end the first phrase in bar 4 on D, and the second phrase on G; the E in bar 3 is my high note. On line two I fill in notes to guide me toward the skeleton, sort of a temporary map. Now I take my idea and fit it on to the map in line three. It's almost okay, but I don't like the way the first two bars fit together, so I move the C that I had planned for bar 2 into bar 1. At this point it sounds good enough to add my chords and see if they work.

 Track 14
line 1

 Track 15
line 2

 Track 16
line 3

 Track 17
line 4

Development of a melodic "skeleton"

INSTRUMENTAL MUSIC

Songs often present themselves instinctively to singers, but instrumentalists sometimes come up with really fine melodies that are not suitable for the voice. Most often this is because there are not enough breaks for the singer to breathe. Sometimes the melody can be adapted by shortening the notes at the end of phrases, but at other times the melody loses too much of its vitality by being broken into phrases like that. If the melody is really good, it is well worth your while to consider whether it could be an instrumental.

Instrumentals seem to have lost a certain amount of their allure since Muzak became associated with some of the worst types of music, but there have been non-vocal hits that range from 1960s songs like "Walk Don't Run," "Wipeout," and "Love Is Blue" to, more recently, the Police's "Behind My Camel" and Rush's "YYZ." Of late, there are lots of examples of classical crossover hits, too.

Melodically an instrumental song is different only by the lack of considering breathing spaces. For your first song, keep it short enough not to tire a performer's fingers, assuming it is for keyboard or guitar. Too much continuous action can also tire a listener's ears. Most instrumentals break up into phrases with cadences that would be suitable for singers, so that some instrumentals (such as "Love Is Blue") can have words added or even start out with words. For reasons mentioned earlier, riff-based songs like "Wipeout" and virtuosic pieces such as "YYZ" are not the best places to start writing songs.

Lacking lyrics, an instrumental must make up for it with a particularly interesting melody. It is all too easy to give up on lyrics and decide to make a song an instrumental, but this is rarely satisfying. However, if the words seem to be only an excuse for the melody, perhaps an instrumental is the proper way to go.

Let's consider a simple piano piece. (The same ideas apply to the guitar, although the limitations of the six strings require dexterity, as well as familiarity with either classical or fingerstyle technique, that is beyond the scope of this book.) For your first song, limit your right hand to the melody, and use your left to provide a simple accompaniment.

On the piano, you have the opportunity for a wider-ranging melody because you are not constrained by the limits of the human voice. But keep in mind that a too-wide melody may be difficult to control and may lead to a disorganized line. You'll make better use of the piano's range if you repeat the melody an octave higher for the second verse; this will also increase the dynamism rather than becoming boring. The same wavelike motions should govern purely instrumental lines. A contrasting section, whether a chorus or not, is still required. If your technique allows and the section is in slower note values, it may be a good idea to play octaves in the right hand to stress the difference.

Despite your level of expertise, a simple accompaniment in the left hand is usually the best idea. A simple pattern of chords, or a bass-chord pattern, will be enough to set off a well-written melody, while even the most complex accompaniments will not hide a deficient one. If you choose a single-note arpeggio pattern, make sure the individual notes do not conflict with the melody. If they do, you might have to change the pattern slightly so that the conflicts are avoided.

If you are interested in writing an instrumental to begin with, read Chapter 5, which looks at one in more depth.

MUSIC FOR GAMES

Music for electronic games is so dissimilar from songwriting that it is rarely discussed at the early stages. Nevertheless, it is built using some of the same principles as regular songwriting, but in different ways with different aims. It may happen that those aims are the exact opposite of what we are looking for in a song, and so we can learn both at once. Even better, you may find that ideas that turn out to be unsuitable for a song end up as perfect game music.

Good game music requires memorable, recognizable themes. They may be as short as a bar or two and are often single phrases; we develop them differently from songs. The form of the music will be dictated by the game's action, and we have no control over how long sections may be. A game player may be in a certain section for hours or may breeze through it in minutes. This alone should make the music writer consider whether they have something that can withstand an hour of repetition. The key is subtlety, reflecting the action but not overwhelming it.

We want to avoid strong cadences, so that the music flows in a continuous stream. Harmonic rhythm should be slow, even if the music itself moves quickly. Write ambiguous harmonies or simple melodies that interact to produce indefinite chords. If the melodies are of different lengths, it will take several repeats before they synchronize into the starting pattern. For example, if you can create one seven-bar phrase (maybe melody) that works with one six-bar phrase (perhaps the bass), it will take 42 bars before the starting notes coincide again. For this to work, be sure that no combination will generate harsh dissonances you don't intend or that don't resolve. Use a scale such as the pentatonic (see page 38) that does not have half steps, so that any notes can sound against any others. You might also use the notes of one complex chord and divide them between the melodies. The harmonic sound will be somewhat static, but the changing melodies will provide a feeling of motion.

Obviously, the normal desire for a single high point in a melody is not possible in this situation, so we make a virtue out of a vice by insisting on the repetition; instead of becoming boring, it should build tension. Much of this can be done with harmony, but melodically we build sections of short motives that are repeated, joined with the same type of section but with different motives. We can generate excitement by changing sections at unexpected times. For example, instead of repeating idea A four times followed by B four times, we might repeat idea A three times, then B seven times, followed by A only twice, one B, then the same pattern over again. The pattern should be long enough that it is not easily recognized as a pattern. The player's attention will be on the game, so the pattern need not be as long as it would be in a concert hall, where everyone's attention is solely on the music.

It is beyond the scope of this book to go much further into game music, but if you find your music seems to fit into this genre and you are happy with the finished product of your first song as game music, then you have won twice over: You have completed your first song *and* found your calling in a fascinating field.

The Pentatonic Scale

Complexity for its own sake is counter-productive. Real sophistication comes from mastering the simplest resources and adding to them as needed. The pentatonic scale is one of the simplest resources we have; it is often scorned for that very reason. While any scale of only five notes is technically pentatonic (*penta* means five), we are interested in the one in common use virtually worldwide. In A minor, its notes are A-C-D-E-G. These same notes, rearranged slightly, form the pentatonic scale of its relative major, C major: C-D-E-G-A. Only the tonic note changes, as well as the harmony of course.

This simple scale does more than reduce the number of notes from the major or minor scales. More importantly, it gets rid of the half steps in the scale and thus many harsh dissonances that can occur. This makes it easier to harmonize a melody using this scale. This is helped by its saturating many different types of music from the ultra-sweet Muzak to thrash/speed/death metal, so that most ears readily accept the entire scale over almost any harmonic structure given to it. Much of the "bad blues" I warned against earlier uses (or abuses) this scale, but it is still capable of creating great melodies and is a tool that no songwriter should be without.

You can take advantage of the characteristics of the pentatonic scale even without making it your only melodic material. For example, adding a #4/♭5 (D♯/E♭ in A minor) gives us the blues scale, and that small change alone has provided countless great melodies, riffs, and solos from some of the finest blues and jazz musicians. It has enlivened progressive and mainstream rock as well as the sweetest ballads.

If you use the pentatonic scale and find your melody too bland or sweet, look for spots to introduce an unexpected note from outside the scale. You can make some amazing discoveries this way. But don't go overboard; the strong impression these make is weakened by over-use.

BUILDING EXCITEMENT

Although falling back on formulas can be a bad idea, there are certain ideas that always seem to work no matter how often they are used, as long as they are used well. The chorus is the part of your song the audience must remember; ideally, they should love it so much they have to sing along with you. One way to build excitement into a song and emphasize the chorus at the same time is to build up to it from the end of the verse, or even add a couple of lines that join the verse to the chorus as a "pre-chorus." It's not really part of either, but shouts, "Here comes the chorus! Get ready!"

One effective way to do this, especially if you have been using carefully created arcs of melody, is to abandon the arc and use a "straight-line" approach right into the chorus. You might have a gentle arc leading up, but then suddenly break into repeated notes that increase in speed and move up bar by bar until they reach a high note that begins the chorus. If the words are building in intensity at the same time, the tension is irresistible and the eruption into the chorus can release an enormous amount of energy.

The following silly example shows how this can work, although you will be able to find many terrific songs that do the same sort of thing much better. The harmony contributes to the effect, of course, and parallel rising chords would complement the rise in the melody to make the chorus sound even more inevitable. At this point, melodic interest is in the slow rise to what we know is going to be a high point, but we don't yet know where it will end. (For this example, I assume a two-octave vocal range.)

Another reason for this particular example is the way the rise comes out of what might be another verse, or even the second half of the current one. Bar 9 ("Drive me") fits melodically and lyrically with what came before, so that when we start building to the climax with the repeated Cs it is a surprise – as if the verse's rug was yanked out from under us – and we find ourselves moving quickly toward the chorus. The formal designations of verse and pre-chorus are not so easily applied here, because what at first sounds like a chorus is suddenly interrupted to become a lead-in to the chorus.

Track 18 (melody only)
Track 19 (melody & harmony)

WORK ON YOUR MELODY!

Almost every melody goes through several revisions before reaching its final form, so you should expect to refine yours over time. Do not worry if you end up making dozens of changes; as long as each one improves the song even slightly, it is important. Even making it worse will teach you a valuable lesson in what not to do, so don't let these discourage you. This is how we all learn – all *except* those who shy away from or deny mistakes, that is.

First, check the range of your melody. The range from the lowest to highest notes should not be more than about an octave and a 5th. Find the key that best fits your voice (where either the top or bottom note is comfortable for you to sing) and see if you can sing it all the way through. Assuming you have an "average" voice, this will give you a rough idea of whether you have exceeded a normal range. (Professional singers will have more range.)

If your melody spans too large a range and you can't bear to change a note, consider making it into an instrumental. Does it have enough character to stand on its own without words? How does it sound with a minimal accompaniment of strummed or held chords? Do you want to write an instrumental?

If you want to keep it vocal, look for sections that can be dropped an octave without harming the overall idea. For example, imagine that I wrote "Get a New Hat" in C, hoping that my soprano singer could reach the high C. (See the example below.)

Track 20

I soon discover that this is beyond many of the singers who wish to sing this particular tune, and that E is a better key for most singers (and one that suits my own voice). Simply transposing the melody to E makes the problem even worse, though, with a virtually impossible high E in the last bar. To fix this, I drop the melody an octave from bar 7 ("you need to …") to the end. This small change not only ends on a more reasonable note, but it also reduces the overall range to less than an octave (a minor 7th), a plausible range for any singer. I made the change at a spot where the melody originally leapt up a 4th; the drop of a 5th does not harm the melody, but in fact is a nice counter move to the continual motion up to E of bars 1 to 6.

The interplay of melody and harmony can become a source of both inspiration and frustration. If I decide to add more chords to the song here, using a standard progression, I have to adjust the original melody in places to fit with the chords, such as replacing the B on the last beat of bar 1 to C♯ to fit with the A chord. The whole next phrase ("Get a new hat!") has to be changed to fit the chords. Mechanically shifting notes to fit with the chords' notes lost the bluesy feeling of the original. I have to decide whether I like this or not, but first let's look at the melody as it is (the next example).

I check to see whether my melody builds to a high note or circles around constantly, returning to one note. While the addition of more chords to the original disguises it a little, bars 1 to 6 start with – and keep returning to – E, which is the highest note of the melody; the song also ends on this note.

Track 23

So at this point I want to liven the melody up a bit and also introduce a higher note. I choose to use the E minor pentatonic scale, and change the first bar's melody to include a high G♮ (note the key signature). This increases the range slightly, but gives the melody a bluesier sound, especially using the C♮ against the A chord (along with the G♮, which makes it an A7). At the same, time I added a new high note, the G. This is where art and craft meet. Craft shows you the possibilities and the art is in your choices.

Track 24

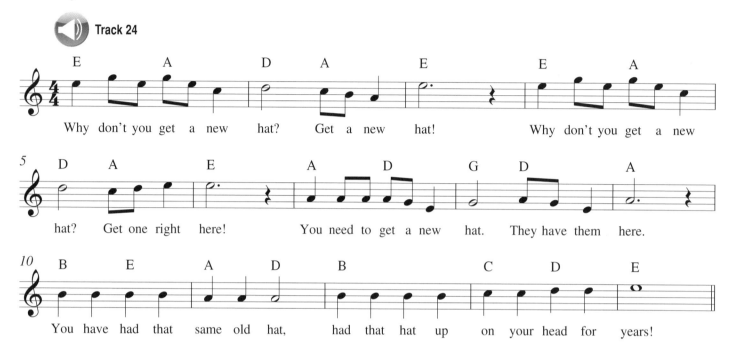

If the interrelation between melody and harmony is obvious, the relation of the melody to the words may not be. Notice that our new high note occurs over relatively unimportant words: "don't" and "get." In this song, the idea of "important" words is stretching the concept a bit, but even here we should practice looking for the best choice. Songwriting is not a deadly serious activity; light, good-natured songs are in demand as long as they are well-written. In this case, the song is about a hat, so that is a good word for a high note. We have several choices, and for now I've decided its first appearance.

Track 25

By changing the first note of bar 2, I felt that I had to lead down to the E in bar 3 by a scale motion. Rather than repeat the A when the phrase recurred in bar 5, I decided to let it stay on D so that there is only one climax note. All this is meant to illustrate options you have. Different choices could have been made at any step and any of those might have been better. One further example shows how you might have chosen a pentatonic chord progression at the start, rather than a major key. This would lend a completely different sound to the song. We will look at this option in more detail in the chapter on Harmony.

Track 26

When you are first getting the hang of shaping a melody, it is a good idea to go through it in this order. When you get more fluent, you can move back and forth between issues of melody and lyrics. For now, check that the accents of the words match the accents of the melody. If the words sound forced or mispronounced, this is the likely cause. In some cases, you can simply move a note on or off a beat; other melodic shapes may require rewriting a phrase altogether. Of course, this applies to most instances, and not where you are going for a special effect. For example, you may be setting the words "I love you" and wish to repeat them, emphasizing each word in turn: "*I* love you… I *love* you… I love *you*." Here the mismatch is used deliberately, to stress the meaning of the common phrase; it makes sense. We want to avoid something like: "Please *give* me a cup *of* sug*ar*," which no melody can make sound natural.

Once you have your lyrics set to your melody, you can start fitting in the chords. Even if you have to change some notes to fit the harmony you want, be sure to keep the accent structure in mind.

CHAPTER 5

SAMPLE INSTRUMENTAL PIECE

Instrumental songs are usually called "pieces" in the classical tradition and many other musicians use this term as well. I use it here because we are not using a lead sheet but the notation that Bach wrote in his instruction book for his wife. (Researchers believe that this piece was written by Christian Petzold, not by Bach, but the master considered it good enough to teach his wife how to play – and possibly how to compose as well.)

For our example, I have chosen just the first half of the minuet because it is virtually a self-contained song. The second half changes key and contains several other technical features that are beyond the scope of this book. If you are interested, you can find the entire piece (and much more free public domain classical music) online at the IMSLP/Petrucci Music Library (imslp.org).

Track 27

Minuet in G

By Christian Petzold

This piece is on two staves, as opposed to the one staff we are using in our lead sheets. Right away, we know that it was meant for keyboard, with the left hand playing the bass clef and the right hand in the treble clef. Although the first beat of the left hand contains a complete chord (G, the tonic), the rest of the left-hand bass part is made up of single notes. These combine with the melody to imply complete chords for every bar.

Let's look at the melody first. A broad overview shows that it is divided into two eight-bar sections by a half cadence at bar 8, and then a full cadence at bar 16. (See Appendix D – Cadence Types – for more information.) Both of these eight-bar sections are divided into four-bar phrases that share rhythmic patterns. You should learn this type of pattern well because it is the basis for a great deal of music in nearly every style.

The first two bars give us the basic idea for the piece, and the general shape of a wave that falls a 5th, then rises back up only to fall again at the end. The same rhythm is repeated in bars 3 and 4, where the melody is changed slightly to accommodate the new chords. These two bars also raise the initial wave from D to a start on E; the wave now rises to the high point of the melody in bar 4. While the upper part of the melody rises, the low note G anchors it.

The second phrase, beginning in bar 5, uses the same rhythmic pattern as bars 1 and 3. This pattern is now used in bars 6 and 7 as well, speeding up the melodic motion and driving us more deliberately toward the cadence in bar 8. This "drive" is relative to the usually relaxed manner in which the piece is most often played, but it is real and an important lesson in creating motion, tension, and release in a melody using rhythm and cadence.

The third phrase, bars 9–12, is a repeat of the first phrase, with the bass becoming more active but still implying the same chords. This is a common technique that helps the ear recognize the melody and join phrases together. Many novice songwriters shy away from exact repetition because they think it shows a lack of inventiveness, but this sort of repeat is ingrained in our ears and sounds natural in most types of music. It is especially useful in more complex music, where the listener has a second chance to make sense of a phrase that might be hard to grasp on first hearing. Remember that without words the ear concentrates more intensely on the melody. Increased bass motion gives it a sense of progressing.

The fourth and final phrase is similar to the second phrase, with changes made in the last two bars to fit in with a full cadence to end the piece. The penultimate bar is cleverly changed so that it forms a sequence with the previous two. As a first song or first piece, this would be a pretty impressive achievement, and 16 bars of this caliber would be enough. If you wanted to write a longer piece, it would be better to use the song forms we discussed earlier rather than continue with the form of a minuet as Christian Petzold did.

The left-hand part (in the bass clef) is a good example of counterpoint, which again is beyond our scope here, so I will keep my discussion of it brief. (For a bit more on contrapuntal techniques, see Appendix E.) It is basically a melody itself, which uses chord tones that are close to one another to form lines that are mostly scale-like or arpeggios (broken chords). We hear these chords with the bass combined with the melody in the treble clef, with the full G chord in bar 1 as a sort of kick-start to the process. The other chords, usually one per bar, are as follows:

Bar 2   G major (G-B-D, B in the bass)

Bar 3   C major (C-E, G implied)

Bar 4   G major (G-B-D, B in the bass)

Bar 5   A minor (A-C, E implied)

Bar 6   G major (G-B, D implied)

Bar 7   Beat 1: D major (D-F♯, A implied)
         Beats 2–3: G major (G-B, D implied and held in the ear from beat 1)

Bar 8   D7 (D-F♯-A-C, a half cadence on V7)

Bar 9   G major (G-B-D, B in the bass)

Bar 10   G major (G-B-D)

Bar 11   C major (C-E, G implied)

Bar 12   G major (G-B-D, B in the bass moving to G)

Bar 13   A minor (A-C, E implied; F♯ bass on beat 3 moving to G)

Bar 14   G major (G-B-D)

Bar 15   Beat 1 Am (A-C, E implied)
          Beats 2–3 - D (D-F♯-A)

Bar 16   G major (B and D implied)

If you are interested in writing this sparse type of texture, with just two notes at a time implying harmonies that contain three (and sometimes four) notes, you should be aware that when a note is omitted from a triad, it is almost always the 5th. This is only common sense, since the root tells you what the chord is, and the 3rd determines whether it is major or minor. The 5th is usually a perfect 5th and is therefore expendable. Of course, it is always possible to add in the 5th at some point in the melody, as Petzold often does in this piece.

The bass part for the first eight bars is a simple scalar melody that breaks the monotony with an arpeggio in bar 7, and then a small run at the end of bar 8 to keep the motion going and lead into bar 9. The second half is similar, using more chord tones to vary the bass part slightly, including the run from bar 8 that shows up again in bar 12. The F♯ in bar 13 could be heard as making a D7 chord, or just as a fancy way of getting to the G in bar 14. As in bar 7, the harmonic motion speeds up in bar 15 to lead to a cadence, this time to a full cadence. The first chord (Am) in bar 15 is obvious, but the next two chords are a sort of shorthand for a common classical cadence formula where the tonic chord appears in second inversion (i.e, with the 5th in the bass), followed immediately by the dominant chord (over the same bass note, here in a different octave), which is completed by the tonic chord in bar 16.

If any of this was difficult to follow, try playing the following version based on what you just read, and then read it again. It should make more sense the second time. (This one-hand version should be playable for keyboard players as well as guitarists.)

Track 28

Much of the bass motion in this piece is used to create a smooth line and relieve the monotony of using the same chord for two bars in a row. It is reasonable to expect musicians who read from a lead sheet to provide a smooth melodic bass line, so what follows is a reasonable lead sheet version. Depending on how much control you want over the bass line, you can use notation such as G/B for bar 2, but it is not strictly necessary. However, it is always the songwriter's prerogative to write out a complete piece such as the original version of the "Minuet in G," if you have the confidence and knowledge to do so. I included the D7 on the last beat of bar 13, but without specifying the F♯ bass, since many bass players (myself included) would play it anyway. (Playing D to G in the bass is too similar to the ending two bars later.)

Track 29 (melody only)

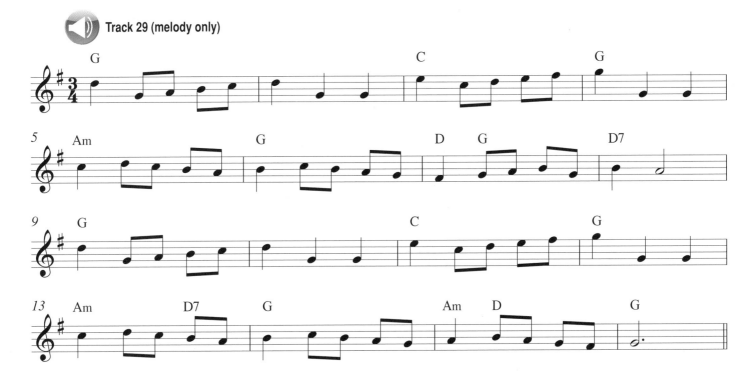

CHAPTER 6

RHYTHM

METER AND RHYTHM

You need to know the difference between meter and rhythm. Meter is the recurring pattern of beats and their accents. Meter forms a background against which rhythm plays. Rhythm is the actual duration of different notes. Many songs are written in the same meter. but few have exactly the same rhythm.

Western culture is surprisingly conservative in its use of rhythm. We might consider our two basic meters to be 2/4 and 3/4. (To read time signatures, the top number tells us how many beats are in a bar, while the lower number tells us what note gets one beat. In both of these, the beat is a quarter note.) Each of these has an accent on the first beat. So the pattern for 2/4 meter is:

ONE-two | ONE-two | ONE-two | etc. (where | denotes a bar line)
meaning
STRONG weak | STRONG weak | STRONG weak | etc.

The pattern for 3/4 (aka "waltz time") is:
ONE-two-three | ONE-two-three | ONE-two-three | etc.
meaning
STRONG weak weak | STRONG weak weak | STRONG weak weak | etc.

All other meters are made up of combinations of these two basic ones, from the most common meter (4/4) to more esoteric ones (5/4, 7/4, etc.). In every meter, we accent the first beat. If we combine 2s and 3s to make a more complex meter, the first beat of each subsequent 2 or 3 gets a bit of an accent, but not as much as the first beat of the bar.

For example, our most common meter 4/4 is like two bars of 2/4: with four beats in a bar, and the quarter note getting one beat. The pattern of accent is:

ONE two Three four | or STRONG weak Medium weak |

Once again, meter and rhythm cannot be separated from all the other aspects of a song, but are strongly dependent on them. The accent in the meter is often slightly louder than the other beats, but it need not be; there are other ways to accent a beat.

In harmony, we normally change chords on the strong beat or beats of a bar, which gives them a subtle accent. Dominant chords on the strong beats create a greater drive to the tonic in a cadence. You can also play around with this by, say, putting a dominant chord on a weak beat for a softer, less definitive cadence to keep from stopping your song prematurely. The same applies to a tonic chord in a cadence ending on the tonic. On a strong beat it tends to resolve fully, while on a weak beat the cadence feels less complete and is easier to continue on from.

A higher note in a melody creates an accent, so high notes often appear on strong beats, particularly when they are to be emphasized, perhaps with an important word in the lyrics. Building a series of melodic arcs that rise to a high point on the first beat of a bar is one powerful technique. This can be enhanced by placing the intermediate high points on weak beats, making the final destination stand out even more. Melodies often start on a strong beat. This is so common that it can become tiresome; because of this, you'll sometimes want to begin a melody on a weak beat (often called an "upbeat").

RHYTHM

The rhythm of a melody reflects the rhythm of the words. While some words may be drawn out to show their importance, straying too far from the natural rhythm of the words tends to sound artsy or even precious. It is important to line up the accents of the words with the accents of the meter; otherwise, the words can sound labored or forced. Sensitivity to the rhythms of music does not automatically translate to sensitivity to the rhythms of words, and vice versa; that's one reason many songwriters team up with lyricists. You should attempt to write lyrics before giving up and searching for a lyricist; like any skill, it takes time and work to master. You probably have spent a great deal of time to master your instrument and/or voice; it will take as much effort to master the art of natural-sounding lyrics. Having said this, it does not take much effort to think of any number of hit songs with lyrics that make little, if any, sense. But this is no excuse for not at least trying to communicate well with your audience. (John Lennon loved to write meaningless words, but the music justified it.) If you are working on your first song, your aim is to write what you consider to be good lyrics, ones that satisfy you as their writer and that communicate with your listeners.

In addition to following the rhythm of the lyrics, there are a few important considerations for rhythm and meter in the words. Your listeners need to know the name of your song so they can request it to be played or search for it online. Tell them the name in the lyrics in a memorable way. This is often done by stating the song's title in an important position in the chorus, where it will be repeated often. The best spot is the beginning of the chorus, which can be highlighted by leading up to it from the verse and stating the title on the strong first beat of the first bar of the chorus. The end of the chorus, and of the song as well, are other great places for the title. Repetition is another way to signal it. The title of "Yesterday" is both the first and last word of the song; it also appears several other times, making it easy to identify.

TIME SIGNATURES AND LYRICS

It is important to fit your words to a rhythm that matches the meter of your song. The most important accent is the first one of the bar. Notice that the same words can fit different meters. In the examples below, the same lyrics are set in both 4/4 and 3/4:

Even without the benefit of melody, the rhythm gives us an idea of how the song might sound. I hear the 4/4 in a medium-slow tempo, a reflective mood, while the 3/4 one is more lively and determined. Notice that, in both versions, the same syllables land on the first beats of the bar; these belong to the most important words in the line.

One reason that 4/4 is our most common time is that 3/4 can become sing-song if the rhythm is all quarter notes and the accents are completely regular, as in:

    YES-ter-day MORN-ing I PIL-fered a BI-cy-cle

    STOLE it from RIGHT un-der OLD Tim-my's NOSE

All the accents are right, but the lyrics sound sing-song because of the straight ONE-two-three pattern over and over again. Nothing stands out; also, "pilfered" is an uncommon word, adding to the forced feeling of the rhythm. Let's look at a song that uses repetitive rhythm creatively.

"Morning Has Broken"

The effect of exact repetition can be wearying or it can be soothing. It all comes down to the melody and how skillfully it is written. A good example of exact repetition of rhythm, which we discussed earlier, is a melody that has been popular for centuries, and one that Cat Stevens made a hit in the 1970s. British author Eleanor Farjeon wrote the words to "Morning Has Broken" in 1931; the tune is the traditional Scottish hymn "Bunessan," which dates from the 19th century or perhaps earlier. It has an unusual, though rigidly maintained, rhythmic pattern.

The hymn is often printed in 3/4 time in modern editions, and is divided into three-bar sub-phrases, which are then grouped into two four-bar phrases. This seemingly unusual grouping is the result of the original actually being in 9/4 time, but with word and melodic accents every three beats, so with the effect of 3/4.

Track 32

"Bunessan" in 3/4 time

Track 33

"Bunessan" in 9/4 time

The 3/4 version takes up 24 bars. The 9/4 version takes only eight bars, but still contains 72 beats (3 x 24 = 9 x 8 = 72). Rhythm ties the whole together, while the change of pitch gives variety; the use of similar pitches also adds coherence. Notice how the longer notes (dotted-half notes) highlight the words they carry (BRO-ken, MORN-ing). The first one seems to have more emphasis because the long note slows down the motion at that point. (If you wanted to accent the second dotted-half note, you could use a leap or a chord change.)

"Bunessan" is an extreme example, but such repetition can work well, with some of the longer notes broken up to accommodate your lyrics. To summarize: Don't throw out lyrics you like because their rhythm starts to sound sing-song; try to create a melody that capitalizes on this instead. Also, consider adding another section with a completely different rhythm as a contrast.

Although the rhythm of your melody will follow the accent pattern of the words, you still have enough leeway to shape it with rhythmic motives of your own. While pitch shapes the outline of melodic waves, rhythm determines how you move through those waves in time. Think of pitch as the height on a graph (the music staff), and rhythm as time it takes the wave to find its shape as the music moves across the page.

PHRASING

We've seen how each bar of a song has meter that determines strong and weak beats. Similarly, phrases of music group into patterns of relatively strong and weak bars. The majority of songs have verses that are eight bars long. These may be stretched to 16 if the music is very fast, but eight is most common. The eight-bar section is usually subdivided into two sections of four bars, with a cadence or rest at the end of bar 4 to give the singer a chance to breathe. (The same pattern is usually found in instrumentals as well.) The four-bar section may be further divided into two sections of two bars, but it is rarely divided into one and three – or three and one. We observe the same division into groups of two that we see in divisions of note values:

Whole note (4 beats) = 2 Half notes (2 beats) = 4 Quarter notes (1 beat)

Even when we subdivide a beat, we continue by twos:

Quarter note (1 beat) = 2 Eighth notes (1/2 beat) = 4 16th notes (1/4 beat) = 8 32nd notes (1/8 beat), etc.

Track 34

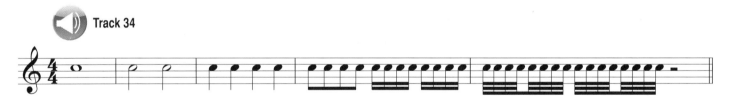

These divisions by two are so common that we need a special notation to divide by three, which you might expect to be common because it is the other of our two basic divisions of meter. However, we need to use triplet notation, as in the following examples, to divide any note values into three:

Track 35

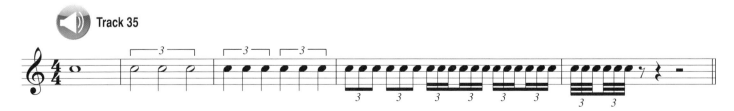

This problem has popped up in different places over the last 500 years, and has often been solved by reinterpreting ordinary "duple" notation as one or another sort of "triple" notation. Most recently, it has surfaced as the notion of "swing" in jazz. (This topic is more complex than we can discuss fully in this book. As with swing, the division has not always been exactly a division into triplets, but it always breaks the notes into a longer one and a shorter one.)

SWING

The most common example of swing in jazz is the interpretation of eighth notes as unequal: the first is lengthened slightly while the second is shortened. This gives a sort of lilting sound to the rhythm, which is more fluid than a strictly regimented, exactly divided series of notes that are each half-a-beat long.

Track 36

This type of reinterpretation has been used since Bach's time, and even earlier. It can seem peculiar to those just learning it, but soon becomes second nature. However, its use is mostly restricted to jazz players, and a more straightforward way of notating this is to make the eighth note the beat, or to make three eighth notes the obvious division of the beat. Using the time signature 12/8 to signify triple division of four beats is the most common way to do this is to, as in this example:

Track 37

Notice that the following two bars sound exactly the same. Although the notation is different, it means the same thing:

Track 38

You can see how 12/8 is simpler to write and to read. Although the eighth note is named as "the beat," we really tend to hear 12/8 as four beats divided into triplets of eighth notes. Time signatures like 12/8 are called "compound meters," in which notes naturally divide themselves into thirds. In compound time, it's the dotted-quarter note that most often represents the beat. Musicians call this the "big beat," so that in 12/8 we have four big beats, in 9/8 we have three big beats, and in 6/8 we have two big beats.

SYNCOPATION

So far we have considered rhythm as placing lyrical accents on metric accents, like the first beat of a bar. Quite often, though, a singer or player will deliberately sing or play slightly before or slightly after the beat. This is syncopation, and it has different effects. If the notes are slightly before the beat or normal placement of the note (half a beat or less), the effect is of urgency or rushing, "pushing the beat." If a note is delayed from its normal placement, the effect is laid back or tentative, "holding back the beat."

If we want to emphasize "troubles" in our earlier example, we could syncopate it so that the syllable appears slightly before the beat, like this:

In this example, we started "troubles" before the first beat of its normal bar. The slight emphasis suggests an urgency about the troubles the singer is portraying.

Syncopation is not necessary for your first song. Still, you need to know what it is in case you find yourself naturally singing that way. I have had students who notated their songs, and were frustrated that the notes they were singing did not fall on the beat they meant for them. When they tapped the beat with their foot, they found that the accent intended for the first beat of a bar occurred when their foot was up in the air *before* it tapped beat 1. Tapping can provide the perfect signal that you are syncopating a note. Similarly, if you tap the beat with your foot and the note comes as your foot rises *after* the beat you thought it was on, you are syncopating after the beat. Both are natural ways of singing and writing.

So if you are notating your song and the melody sounds too stiff or too straight when played as written, you probably have syncopated parts of it. Try the foot-tapping method to find those notes. Although syncopation may sound complex, in actuality it can make the lyrics sound more natural.

TEMPO AND RHYTHM

The chapter on Melody points out the importance of considering the tempo of our song and the effect it has on the rhythm. Indicate the speed using words like allegro, andante, fast, slow, etc.; use a metronome marking to be even more precise. Time signatures help, too. For example, we might use 12/8 to indicate a moderate-to-slow bar of four beats divided into threes. This is only a rough approximation, but you should be sure to keep track of the tempo, not only of your finished song, but of your ideas as well. Many ideas sound best at a certain tempo; if you forget that fact, you might throw away a good idea because you later tried to sing it at the wrong speed.

CHAPTER 7
HARMONY

Along with lyrics and melody, your song needs an indication of the chords that accompany them. Some songwriters devise more or less elaborate accompaniments to their songs, but this is a separate skill that should be worked on after you are capable of writing a good basic song. A good song can stand on its own, even with long-held chords or simple strumming. No amount of arrangement can redeem a poor melody, although it may be able to cover it up; in such a case, it is really the accompaniment that is interesting. (Refer to the examples on page 16.)

There are many choices for harmony, so our goal is to select chords that set off our melody best, that set the mood we want, and that please us rather than following some rule book.

You may choose to write your entire melody and then harmonize it, but more often songwriters harmonize as they go. Sometimes you may even sing over a series of chords and derive your melody that way. All these methods point to the interdependence between the melody and harmony. The chords can change the meaning of even a simple melody. For example, consider this four-note motive:

If we want a single chord to cover this entire bar and even suggest what follows, we have several options. Let's look at three of the simplest. Here, PT = passing tone.

Using a G major chord starts us off on a chord tone, and each strong beat contains a chord tone. The weak beats are passing tones that connect chord tones into a smooth scalar line. (If you are unfamiliar with passing tones, appoggiaturas, etc., see Appendix E.) This chord implies that the first melody note in the next bar will be a G.

But a G chord is not the only option.

If we choose F, the strong beats now have passing tones and the weak beats have chord tones. Passing tones that appear on strong beats and lead into chord tones are usually called "appoggiaturas," which simply means "leaning notes;" they are notes that "lean into" chord tones on the next beat. Play the example slowly on your instrument and you will feel how the strong beats resolve onto the weaker ones. This is a different result from having chord tones on strong beats; it seems to give the music an extra push to move it along. This is a valuable effect to know about. Notice that this example uses an F as the first note of the next bar. This is not strictly necessary, and we could continue using appoggiaturas into the next bar, but they have to stop at some point; the start of a bar can be a convincing place to do that. It gives it a bit more emphasis.

As shown in the example below, harmonizing the bar with C leaves us with only one chord tone, and that one on a weak beat. The bar starts with an appoggiatura that leads to C, and then two consecutive passing tones lead into the next chord tone, on the downbeat of bar 2. Remember that our harmonic system is triadic, so if we use a triad and add the root on top, there is a 4th between the chord's 5th (G) and the upper octave root (C). This gap of a 4th requires two passing tones to fill it. This is another effect that is important to know about, since the melody almost floats above the harmony, only "touching down" on the note C until it gets to the next bar and lands on G.

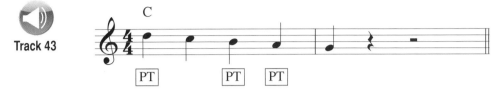

Those are just three of the possible chords we could choose for this motive, and we used only major triads! See how many other major triads you can find that will fit the tune. Listen to the effect they have and the notes needed to start the next bar. Then do the same with minor chords. For extra interest, try 7th chords. You may be surprised at the sounds you can get just by adding the 7th to a chord. As just one example, let's try using D7:

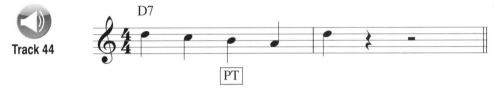

In this case, there is only one passing tone since D, C, and A are all chord tones. (The D in the following bar is only one of many choices you have.) Because the 7th is only a step away from the tonic note, the first two notes in this step-wise progression belong to the same chord and do not need a passing tone. It makes sense that if you have a seven-note scale and a three-note chord, then there are four notes that do not belong to the chord. If the chord has four notes (like D7), then only three scale notes are not in it. A five-note chord such as a full 9th chord is missing only two of the scales notes. A full 13th chord would contain the entire scale.

"CLASSICAL" HARMONY

If you have studied "classical harmony" or a course based on it, you are liable to have the impression that harmony is a series of rules that suck the life out of music. It is often taught that way, but we will approach it from a modern songwriter's point of view. It's not even that the *rules* have changed as much as our *goals*, which are now so different that most of the rules are no longer relevant. There are many ideas and conventions from classical theory we want to keep because they are the most specific way to talk about notes and chords. The main thing we need to jettison is the notion that rules must be followed to make valid music.

What has remained constant for centuries: note names; intervals; keys and key signatures; meter and time signatures; note durations; treble and bass clefs; and most other commonly used notation. New additions include guitar tablature, guitar chord diagrams, and special performance instructions for techniques like bending guitar strings, plucking the strings of a piano, generating harmonics on a piano, playing behind the bridge on a violin, etc. New instruments have their own vocabulary.

The most obviously irrelevant rules forbid movement in consecutive parallel 5ths or octaves, the complete contents of "power chords" and the basis of all barre chords on the guitar as well as left-hand technique of many piano styles. They are so much a part of the musical soundscape that we rarely pay attention to them, nevermind hearing some broken rule.

Other "rules" only outline tendencies of tones to move the shortest distance, such as the leading tone rising a semitone to the tonic, or the 7th of V7 to fall by semitone to the 3rd of the tonic. "Tendency" simply means they most often do this, but don't have to. Whether a song works is up to you and your listeners.

Many first-time songwriters make a big mistake by trying to be too harmonically sophisticated. It is enough to be able to combine words, melody, and harmony into one coherent, meaningful whole. Certainly you should use any chords you are comfortable with and that suit the song, but remember that the song is not a harmony exercise. The chords are there to support the melody and to intensify the words. One or two "advanced" chords can sound out of place and ruin the balance of a song.

MINOR KEYS

A good portion of basic music theory can be found in this book's appendices, but we need to take a close look at the minor keys. They are poorly understood, even by many teachers, and are often taught poorly as a result. This section is how I wish I had been taught.

If you have learned that there are four minor scales for each minor key, the typical approach, I intend to show you that there is only one. The minor scale changes under certain conditions and they all relate to a single problem – the leading tone. Minor keys share a key signature with their relative major (which is what makes them "relatives"), but they need an additional change: They need to raise the 7th of the scale so that it is half step below the tonic and acts as a true leading tone. If you have wondered why this need has not been addressed by simply adding that sharp, natural, or double-sharp to the key signature, then you know that this is rarely, if ever, discussed. So let's discuss it. First, let's look at the chords of the key of A minor (since like its relative major, C major, it has no sharps or flats):

The first thing that stands out is that some chords (V and the second version of vii) have G♯, while others (III and the first version of vii) have G♮. The G♯s are easy to understand: A dominant chord needs the leading tone and the diminished chord on the leading tone obviously does, too. Many harmony books show III as an augmented chord, but this is simply adding the leading tone idea to III. The augmented chord is almost never used in classical compositions or songs, while the major chord on III is the relative major chord that shows up all the time. In fact, this chord makes it simple to move back and forth between relative minor and relative major; the diminished chord on ii functions as vii in the relative major and helps get us there while still just using chords in the key of A minor.

The first version of VII is a major chord; it is used a lot in both folk and rock. It can function as the dominant of the relative major and makes it even easier to move between keys; combined with the notes of ii, it forms V7 of the relative major. We have two useful versions of the vii chord, and we need both G and G♯ for them.

So if minor harmony is so simple, why the complication about scales? Let's look at the scale we get from the chords. Since by definition (or rule) a diatonic scale has only one version of each of the seven steps, we have to choose G or G♯. Since we must have a leading tone, we have to use G♯ in our scale:

The problem occurs between notes 6 and 7, in A minor between F and G♯. Remember (or check Appendix B) that scale tones have to be major or minor 2nds, either a whole step or half step apart. Since F to G♯ is three half steps, it is an augmented 2nd, an interval *forbidden* by music theorists and usually avoided by composers. Something has to change, and since a leading tone must be a half step below the tonic, F must change to become F♯. This way, it is a whole step away from both E and G♯. So great, right? Problem solved. Except that F♯ turns the major chord VI into a diminished chord, and one that leads to G major (where it is vii). This inconvenient situation was solved by using F♯ when a melody goes up to G♯, usually as a passing tone where it does not disturb the harmony. If the leading tone is not needed, as when using iii or the other version of vii, the G♮ doesn't require changing the F at all, so it remains F♮. These notes also remain just G and F when the melody falls, say as A-G-F-E.

Most theorists decided they needed four scales to account for this simple adaptation to the leading tone. The scale in the example above was called the harmonic minor scale, because it was derived from the chords, although most textbooks turn this inside out and say that the chords are derived from the scale. Because F becomes F♯ before G♯, but stays F after G♮, theorists created the melodic minor scale that has two forms: the *ascending melodic minor scale* raises both 6 and 7 (F♯ and G♯ in A minor), while the *descending melodic minor scale* lowers them (back to plain F and G in A minor). Finally, the *natural minor scale* is the minor scale with only the notes of the key signature, with no leading tone (exactly the same as the descending melodic minor scale). In actual practice, you may want to raise F to F♯ before G♯ (in A minor), and if so that's really all you need to remember. Many songwriters like the sound of F-G♯ and use the "harmonic" minor scale for melodies as well. It's up to you.

USING ROMAN NUMERALS

We will refer to chords by name, and also by Roman numerals, when dealing with chords built on scale steps, regardless of key. So if appropriate, we might call a chord F, or we might label it IV (F, in the key of C major) to denote the chord built on the fourth scale step of any major key. We use lower-case Roman numerals to refer to minor chords, such as iv for the fourth step in a minor scale (Fm, in the key of C minor). We use upper-case for major and augmented chords, lower-case for minor and diminished chords. (Appendix C has more on triads.)

The most important chords in a key are I, IV, and V. In the key of C, these are C, F, and G; in the key of G, they are G, C, and D; and in A minor they are Am, Dm, and E. They are important because, between them, they contain every note in the scale and can be used to harmonize any note in the key. If a song sticks to the scale, these are the only chords needed. They may not be the only chords used, since others may be employed for variety or color or any other reason. But if you are stuck for a chord to use for a particular melody note, one of these three chords will work.

"My Bonnie Lies Over the Ocean" (see page 27) is a good example of a song that can be harmonized with just I, IV, and V – in this case C, F, and G. The verse consists of four phrases. The first rocks from I to IV and back to I (a mild move), while the second phrase progresses from I to IV and ends with a half cadence on G. Phrase 3 repeats the first phrase, and phrase 4 ends the verse with a strong full cadence IV-V-I (F-G-C). This simple chord progression is suitable for a folk song; it was also made popular in the 20th century because it works under a boogie beat.

Even in this simple song we can see the difference between using chords for supporting the melody versus chords that progress using tendency tones. The F chord of bar 2 supports the melody notes, and its mild motion away from the tonic C is immediately cancelled by the return to C in the next bar. The next four bars *progress* by moving away from C to F and pushing forward to G, where we pause but feel that we have to continue: The leading tone in the harmony (not in the melody) urges us to resolve it to the tonic C chord. This tendency is made more obvious and more urgent at the end of bar 14 where the leading tone in the melody requires the resolution to the tonic chord to support the melodic resolution to the tonic note.

The regular change of chords allows the F chords to harmonize the note D in bars 2 and 10, where the D quickly moves to C (a chord tone). This same thing works on bars 20 and 28 of the chorus, where D is the only note in the bar. This time it is a combination of the echo of the upward-moving 4th in the melody from G to C, then A to D. The ear expects to hear D in the melody, but it also expects the F chord to last for two bars, so it sounds "right" even though D is not part of an F chord. This is an important lesson to digest. Melodic and harmonic expectations can trump "theoretically correct" ideas and actually sound better.

Chord substitution is often considered a complex subject, but at its core it is just finding a different chord to harmonize a note than the one commonly used. In songwriting you will often use it without the fancy name because you are dissatisfied with the obvious chord, or the one you have originally chosen. Let's say you are writing "My Bonnie Lies Over the Ocean" and are not happy using F in bar 6, a reasonable possibility since it was used in bar 2 and is coming up again in bar 10. The F chord harmonizes the note C; what other chord does that, too? C does (C-E-G), although it has just been used. A minor (A-C-E) is a possibility. Going one step further harmonically, D7 would work as well (D-F♯-A-C). These are all good, but produce different effects. A minor gives a softer sound, one that fits well with the folk idiom. It also is in the key, and is often used as a substitute for C because it has two common notes. The D7 introduces a note from outside of the key (F♯), and it is the V7 of G. This adds strength to the cadence on G in bar 7, and also harmonizes all the notes in bar 13 as well as strengthening that cadence. Again, it depends on the sound you like. One more point in favor of the D7 is that it could substitute for the F chords in the chorus if you like the sound. Try these yourself and see which you prefer.

The process for finding possible substitute chords: Determine the note you are harmonizing, and find the chords in which it is the root, 3rd, 5th, 7th. Try them all and then let your ear decide.

Place cadences properly. Base them on pauses for the singer as well as the flow of the melody. Usually there will be a half cadence part way through a verse or chorus, and a full cadence at the end. In longer sections there may be several half cadences. Be careful not to have too many full cadences; they will give your harmony a stop-start-stop-start jerkiness that can undermine even a good melody.

If you add harmony to an existing melody, be careful not to overdo it. You do not have to harmonize each and every note. As we have seen, quite often one chord will harmonize several notes, a complete bar, or even several bars. It is more important to have a consistent rate of chord change for a song than for every note to fit perfectly into every chord. In fact, a consistently changing series of chords can often lull the ear into accepting the notes that would not sound quite right in isolation, as we saw in "My Bonnie." Change chords mostly at even intervals, perhaps speeding up the changes to lead to a high point or ending, but otherwise at a constant rate.

Harmonic rhythm is the term for how often chords change. A consistent length of time between chord changes gives a song a polished feel. In "My Bonnie," the chords change almost every bar in the verse, whereas in the chorus they change every two bars. This gives the chorus a more laid-back, expansive feeling. Once you have felt this, go back to the verse and notice how the spots where chords are held for two (and even three) bars relax any feeling of motion or tension, while the subsequent bars that speed up to one bar per chord have a stronger feeling of progression. This is not immediately obvious, especially to an untrained listener, but it gives the songwriter a lot of power in setting a mood and subtly manipulating it.

LEAVING THE KEY

In the early stages of songwriting, it is usually advisable to stick to a single key or a scale for your melody. As we saw in the chapter on Melody, notes from outside the key stand out. They can be useful to draw attention to the note after them, but often require chords from outside the key as well.

Let's say you have tried using the major chords of a key, and then substituting minor chords where possible. If you still feel the song needs one or more new chords, you can "borrow" them from the parallel key. It has the same name, but is in the opposite mode; e.g., C minor is the parallel minor to C major. If you write a song in C major, you can use chords from C minor if they fit with your melody. In this case, besides C minor itself, the most useful chords are Fm (iv) and A♭ (VI). Look at the following example, from a song that could be called "Leaving Home." The first version uses only chords from C major, and sounds pretty static, like we haven't really gone anywhere:

Track 45

If we simply change the last chord, we can give the impression that we have left the "home" of C without even changing the melody. Listen to the difference achieved by changing this one chord to A♭:

Track 46

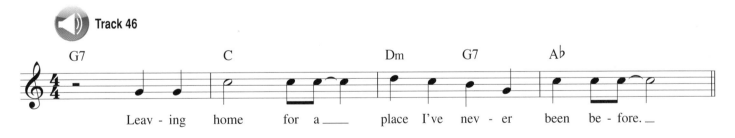

Although we have changed just the chord, it sounds like "a place [we've] never been before." It works because the melody note C is the 3rd of A♭.

Many songs use this type of chord borrowing. In "Desperado" by the Eagles (in the key of G major), the third chord is the regular IV (C), but the fourth chord is the iv borrowed from G minor (Cm), on the word "senses." It adds depth to the song with a melody in G and harmony that borrows a note from the parallel minor.

HARMONIC PROGRESSIONS

Your melodies are supported by chords. Unless you are writing something like "Three Blind Mice," you will need more than one chord. The chords should have a sense of motion that we call *progression*. This sense of motion is achieved by using chords that move away from the tonic and then back toward it. Simple progressions get back to the tonic quickly, while complex progressions tend to have more secondary destinations on the way. (Our examples use just chord names, since the voicing of the chords is not relevant to the discussion; you decide how to play them.)

A sense of motion is created by moving away from the tonic and then back toward it. Chords V and vii have a strong pull back to the tonic, while the other triads all move away from I; vi and iii are mild, while IV and ii are more distant feeling. (We will explore these more.) Motion is also created when dissonance resolves to consonance. In both these cases, a sense of instability moves to a sense of stability. Note that too much stability sounds dull, a sense of going nowhere.

Working chord by chord is a common mistake made by songwriters at every level, especially when faced with writer's block. This is to music what jigsaw puzzles are to painting. As a songwriter, you want to understand series of chords as units, units that progress from one place to another, and which carry the melody along with them. For example, taking each chord as one full bar, G-C-G is a simple move away from G and back. G-D-G is a similar motion, but the pull back is stronger, and G-D7-G is stronger yet. The dominant chord moves strongly to the tonic and the V7 moves even more strongly. Try it yourself.

 Track 47

Subdominant, Dominant, and Tonic Progressions

The progression G-C-D moves away from the tonic to C, then further away to D. If we stop there, we have a half cadence, like a breathing point or a comma in a sentence. We can't stop on D, though, so we progress onward to G. Moving from D-G or D7-G gives us a full cadence, or full stop, just like a period in a sentence.

Now let's take the progression G-C-G-D-C-D-G in the key of G. This common chord sequence is found in many songs in different keys at differing speeds. We can think of it in two distinct parts: G-C-G-D and C-D-G.

It starts with the tonic chord G, moves mildly away to C, slides back to the tonic and then moves farther away to D, the dominant. This half cadence leaves us expecting a move back to G. The second part surprises us a bit by going to C instead of G, but then it moves back to D, which finally resolves to G. This C-D-G movement replaces a simple G chord, drawing out the resolution from the D at the end of part one to the G at the end of part 2. This simple three-chord progression both increases the tension and then resolves it. It is often repeated to emphasize the resolution with a sort of "echo" effect. You can either repeat lyrics in the echo, write new ones, or repeat the melody instrumentally. All of these work well.

We have used seven chords. If we use each for a whole bar and want an eight-bar melody, this requires one more chord at the end. If this is the end of the song, we can repeat the G to give an air of finality. Otherwise, we can keep the harmony moving by setting up another C-D-G progression and adding Em, for example, which fits nicely between G and C. This gives us several choices, one of which is:

G | C | G | D | C | D | G | Em | C | D | G | G ||

 Track 48

We want to write our melodies over entire progressions, so they fit the movement of the chords. Often, a chord progression will help guide a melody that doesn't sound quite right. A solid progression can keep a melody on track, rather than rambling aimlessly. It can also suggest the continuation for a melody that is under construction. Where the melody is complete, there are many different chords to choose from for each melody note. Strong progressions will support the melody while weak ones will undermine it. Common guides to creating solid progressions, which have often hardened into rules in teaching, concern the use of all seven triads of the major key – and for more advanced or richer harmony also include the 7th chords built on them.

The tonic chord I is usually the goal of a progression. It may be temporarily denied to increase harmonic tension, usually by using vi (e.g., Am in C major). This chord shares two of its notes with the C major triad: the tonic note C and its major 3rd E (suggesting C major, not C minor). The chords built on scale steps IV and ii (F and Dm in C major) are called subdominant chords; these most effectively move to the dominant chord V. The dominant chord V and the rarely used diminished chord on vii lead strongly to I.

In a major key, the major chords have the strongest functions, while the minor chords are used for variety and to substitute for major chords in specific situations. Using progressions that move from subdominant to dominant to tonic (SD-D-T) is a good rule of thumb for a beginner, or for anyone experiencing a frustrating mental block. SD-D-T is the backbone of our common progression:

    G (T)-C(SD)-[G(T)]-D(D)-C(SD)-D(D)-G(T) or I-IV-I-V-IV-V-I.

 Track 49

The third chord is not strictly necessary; there are many songs that use the progression without that chord. (Now you can see why both work.) In C major, the progression would be:

    C-F-G-F-G-C

We can also use two chords for each function. In this case, it is most effective to use the major chord first. Let's do this with the progression in C major:

    C-Am-F-Dm-G-G7-C

Track 50

This progression has several interesting features. The first four chords have roots that progress by descending 3rds, suggesting a smooth bass line with the use of passing tones (in parentheses) between the roots:

    C-(B)-A-(G)-F-(E)-D

The bass then descends a 5th, the strongest root movement, to the dominant chord G. The G7 can be considered a combination of the V and vii chords, or just a stronger version of V. Either way, it intensifies the need for resolution back to the tonic.

Of course, not every major chord needs to be followed by its minor functional equivalent, and parts of this progression are the basis of thousands of songs. This doo-wop and early rock 'n' roll standard is one version:

    C-Am-F-G

Track 51

Another is the standard jazz formula:

(C)-Dm-G-C (commonly called a "ii-V-I")

 Track 52

SD-D-T progressions always sound right, whereas a D-SD progression can sound off-kilter in many situations, even to a casual listener. This should not be considered a rule, however, because there are situations where a dominant chord goes to a subdominant chord quite successfully. The basic blues progression is the most outstanding example. In C, it looks like this:

C7-F7-C7-C7-F7-F7-C7-C7-G7(D)-F7(SD)-C7-G7

 Track 53

This works because our ears are used to this particular progression, and we have grown to expect it. (Early objections to blues were precisely due to this "backward" harmonic movement, as well as the use of unresolved dominant 7th chords.) Another example is our G-C-G-D-C-D-G, where the 5th chord C (SD) has moved back from the dominant (D) as if to "take a run" at the full cadence C-D-G. We hear it as two motions, G-C-G-D and C-D-G. So while the progressions SD-D-T or just D-T are not rules, you should know when your progressions don't follow these common patterns; you should have good reasons for not doing so. Quite often, a problem with a song can be traced back to inadvertently violating the expectations set up by these patterns.

In general, these same expectations hold in minor keys. The diminished chord on ii is most often used in jazz, although some pop ballads use it successfully as well. Remember that VI is a major chord in a minor key (A♭ in C minor); it is useful in producing variety, especially when the tonic C minor is expected.

Fifth Progressions

Bass movement by 5th is possibly the most important type of progression. We do not have space to explain all the acoustic reasons our ears hear the bass dropping a perfect 5th as the strongest harmonic motion. For now, let's just say that this is the strongest harmonic (overtone) and is the note most strongly tied to the tonic. This is the reason the dominant chord is the one a 5th above the tonic. Other progressions where the chord's bass drops a 5th (or rises a 4th) are strong as well, and a chain of them forms a strong progression. We have already seen that ii-V-I is a basic progression in jazz; the bass moves by a 5th between each of these chords. You can extend this progression to vi-ii-V-I or iii-vi-ii-V-I or even vii-iii-vi-ii-V-I, although the vii-iii progression uses the diminished vii chord.

The IV chord is omitted because IV-vii is a diminished 5th bass motion. This is not quite so strong, although it has become common in jazz and progressive rock. However, we can continue our sequence of perfect 5th motions with vii-iii-vi-ii-V-I-IV, where IV is a perfect 5th below the tonic. This subdominant chord is like a dominant (or perfect 5th) from the tonic, but from below. This gives us another insight into why the SD-D-T progression seems so natural; we are balancing the tonic by approaching it first from below, and then from above.

Returning to our 5th motion, the previous examples are all diatonic progressions because they use only the notes of the key. In the key of C, our full example would be Bdim-Em-Am-Dm-G7-C-(F). G7 is added to point out the special attraction V7 has to the tonic, due to the 5th motion, the leading tone, and the 7th. We could change our diatonic progression to a *chromatic* one by making *all* of the chords dominant 7ths: B7-E7-A7-D7-G7-C. In each case, they almost resolve to the next chord, but that chord turns out to be a V7 that has to be resolved, and the chain continues until it finally does resolve on C. (As an aside, this type of progression can continue through all 12 tones as a true chromatic progression, returning to its starting point: B7-E7-A7-D7-G7-C7-F7-B♭7-E♭7-A♭7-D♭7-G♭7-B7(C♭7). Technically, the last chord is C♭7, which is the same as B7.)

I mention the chromatic progression only for completeness and do not recommend it for your first songs; it strays far from the original key and can be difficult to fit a melody to. For example, in E7-A7-D7-G7-C, the E7 contains G♯, which contradicts the dominant note G; the A7 has C♯ which contradicts the tonic. The diatonic progression is much more useful at first.

Pentatonic Progressions

While *rock 'n' roll* tends to use the three major chords of the major scale, showing its roots in country and blues music, *rock* tends to use progressions from the minor pentatonic scale. The chords are still often major, although the 3rd can be omitted to form a bare 5th or "power chord," but they are usually based on I, ♭III, IV, V, ♭VI, and ♭VII. In the key of C: C, E♭, F, G, A♭, and B♭. Heavier music adds half step motion to the chords, so in C again add D♭ and G♭. For example, if we transpose these chords to the key of G, we get: G, A♭, B♭, C, D♭, D, E♭, and F, which Deep Purple used to create "Smoke on the Water," inspiring hundreds of metal bands.

Descending Bass Progressions

Many progressions are built over the descending bass line C-B-A-G. These can be diatonic, such as C-G/B-Am-G7 or more chromatic – e.g., C-G-D7/A-G7. The bass that leads this type of progression can be extended to C-B-B♭-A-G or C-B-A-A♭-G to amplify the number of harmonic options. Experiment with the different chords that fit over these bass lines. Try the same thing with the similar bass C-B♭-A♭-G. While the bass leads the progressions, they can still follow 5th progressions – remember that it is the chord root that progresses by 5th, not necessarily the bass note! – or SD-D-T progressions, with the tonic being added at the end. The familiarity and solidity of the repeating bass can allow great latitude in the chords on top.

MUSIC FOR GAMES

Music for electronic games is covered in the chapter on Melody. Harmonically, this genre is best kept simple, especially when beginning to learn the art and craft of it. Because there will be a lot of repetition, cadences should not attract attention. The simplicity of much early game music is not necessarily due to a lack of skill, but rather the realization that a theme may be repeated almost endlessly. A few simple phrases with a single chord or two, if done well, can bear more repetition than a complex harmonic construction that will tire the ear.

Whereas a normal song looks for breathing space for the singer and provides cadences at these points, game music is continuous, without the need for "punctuation." In fact, it is best to start by completely avoiding common cadence formulas like V7-I. Many game themes hover around tonic, which can be approached simply from vi, IV, or iii without drawing the ear's attention.

When designing music for other-worldly settings, it makes sense to look for unusual combinations of notes, forming chords that are beyond the scope of this book. In fact, a good rule of thumb is not to base your chords on 3rds, like most other music is. If you come up with a chord such as C-D-F-G that you cannot name but seems to fit the game, use it.

EXPANDING STANDARD PROGRESSIONS

The pentatonic scale (see page 38) accompanied by the 12-bar blues progression is a common combination. Over time, this merger has become stale through overuse. If you have already started your harmonic accompaniment this way, you can salvage it by inserting progressions that support the structure but delay its expectations. "Day Tripper" by the Beatles is a good example of expanding the structure. (Listen to the chord expansion on the audio track.)

 Track 54

"Day Tripper" is based on a riff that is a decorated arpeggio of the tonic chord E. Its chords follow the predictable move to A and then back to E, but before proceeding to the expected B the song moves to F♯. This is a surprise, but not a big one because it is the dominant of B; when followed by A, though, it creates excitement as it frustrates our expectations. With the move to G♯, we may wonder what to expect at all, at least until it moves to C♯. Then, even if only subconsciously, our ears hear that we are in a Cycle of 5ths (G♯-C♯-F♯-B) that will go back to the tonic E. Harmonic excitement is ramped up by skipping the F♯ and moving directly from C♯ to B and then returning to E with the riff. The beauty of music is that even for such a condensed version of the harmonic structure, it takes all these words to describe what happens musically in a few seconds.

So what did Lennon and McCartney do? They started with a standard blues progression, giving us enough of it to expect the move to B. Then they delayed it by seeming to go to its dominant, but extended that progression. As a final harmonic coup, just when our ears thought they knew what to expect, they left out a chord to hurry to the expected B to surprise us one last time.

There are a couple of lessons for us here:

1. Delay expectations by adding chords. This works particularly well with the blues progression, since it is a 12-bar structure while most others are eight- or 16-bar constructions. Many times we can add four bars without upsetting the harmonic balance, adding interest for the listeners.

2. When leading up to a climax on an expected chord, it is powerful to speed up the harmonic motion, either by changing chords more quickly or – in the case of "Day Tripper" – by leaving out one of the chords in a progression. This type of harmonic device is useful with any standard chord progression.

COMBINING SCALES IN ONE KEY

While most songs stick to one key – or one type of key, such as major – some chart-busting songs combine different versions of the key. For example, "Sgt. Pepper's Lonely Hearts Club Band" begins with pentatonic harmony and the defining chord progression in rock music (G-B♭-C-G), but the middle section (where the horns come in) is written in pure major. The contrast is intentional, giving the listener an idea of the mixture of styles and textures to come on the album. The rockier version of the song ("Reprise") sticks to the pentatonic scale for a more hard-edged feel, perfect for leading into the dreamy and introspective finale.

Another classic example is W.C. Handy's "St. Louis Blues." This little masterpiece is in three parts: It begins in G minor, then switches to a standard blues progression (still in G) before ending in a blues-inflected G major. The final section is possibly the most interesting harmonic area of the song, combining the harmonic ideas of the first two parts.

Be aware of the effects that a given scale – or certain scales in combination – can produce. While writing a happy song in a minor scale is a worthy challenge, it might be better to master writing sad songs first – before trying to discover how to use the same materials for the opposite effect.

Example – "Get a New Hat"

In "Get a New Hat," my first harmonization was somewhat bluesy. Every note in the melody belongs to the chord that harmonizes it:

Track 55

I could also use a more pentatonic harmony to create a riff-like progression that might be useful if I want something closer to a rock sound:

Track 56

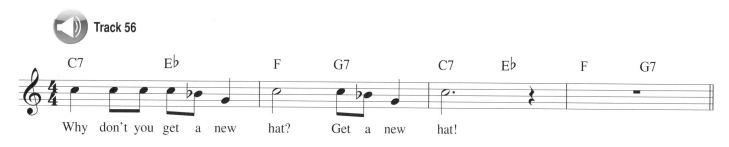

Now the notes don't fit the chords so neatly, but they still sound fine. (I had to add a bar of rest to complete the chord progression, which also makes the three-bar phrase into a more conventional four-bar one, and gives the singer a rest.) The E♭ chord works well because the C sounds okay against it, and the other two notes are part of the chord. Even if the C clashed a bit with the chord, it would still work because it immediately resolves to the B♭ of the chord. The trickiest part is the G7 chord, but it works because our ear has just heard C go to B♭, so it is the B♭ that sticks out. As we have seen, B♭ is a blue note against a G7 chord; it has the great bluesy sound that rock has borrowed from blues. The melody resolves to C and the chords repeat.

Alternatively, we could surprise the listener by starting with what seems like a blues 7th chord, but then cadencing in the key of F. This reveals the C7 as V7 of F all along:

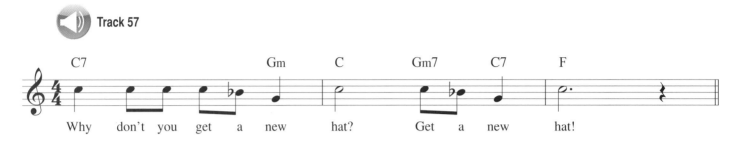

Track 57

This example shows several things. The harmonic rhythm does not have to be constant, especially if we have an effect in mind that overrides it, such as the sudden cadence at bar 3. Although it is in the key of F, we did not start off on the tonic chord or note, which contributes to the little surprise of landing on F. Most importantly, it shows that there are many possibilities for harmonizing even this simple three-bar phrase. The craft of songwriting means you see how many possibilities there are and what they are. The art lies in choosing the one that best suits your song. Only you can decide that.

CONTINUE TO WRITE A SONG!

Look over your own song so far. If you have a melody, try to harmonize it with just three chords, keeping the progression SD-D-T in mind. Does that improve it? Try adding alternate chords to see if these sound better. Experiment with all the chords from the key. Try the chords from the parallel major or minor. If you feel daring, try to add one chord from outside of the key.

Once you have chords that harmonize your melody, check them to be sure that they progress. Not every progression has to be by 5th or SD-D-T or any other standard one, but be aware of the motion in your song and why it is as it is. For example, a love song might have long stretches of chords that move away from the tonic, giving a floating feeling to the harmony – one that should be reflected in the words and melody as well. An angrier, more aggressive song could have frequent strong cadences, as if to underline tough statements and short outbursts.

For your first song, try to have lyrics, melody, and harmony all working in sync to produce a strong effect. This is enough of a challenge right now. Later you may wish to have them contradict one another for parts of a song – as a special effect or to highlight part of the lyrics – but for now, master the basics. That's a tall enough order.

CHAPTER 8

LISTENING LIKE A SONGWRITER

We all have several different roles in our lives. These require different skills, both technical and social. "Songwriter" is a role, as well as a calling or hobby. As such, it requires technical knowledge as well as social interaction. Your goals and ambitions dictate how much of each.

You will need confidence, a trait most new songwriters lack, despite any bravado they may show. The purpose of this book is to instill in you that confidence by writing your own good song. That changes you.

You need to learn the basics of how music works, specifically from the perspective of writing a popular song. This is indispensable, and the earlier you learn it, the sooner you will be writing quality material. You may know someone who is "self-taught" who has done just fine so far. Do you wish you had taught yourself to read? Have you ever tried to teach yourself a foreign language? There are many things you can learn a lot faster when taught systematically, and music is one of them.

Beyond the theory of scales and chords, you need to learn the expectations your musical ideas set up; only then can you fulfill them to your own satisfaction and to that of your audience. Once you know how to do this, you can start experimenting with those expectations to heighten an effect. In their song "Bravest Face," Rush does this masterfully. A heavy electric intro quickly gives way to a jazzy acoustic section that seems incongruous. The song turns out to be about the two sides to everyone and every situation, and how you might as well show "your bravest face" in adversity. Technical similarities hold the song together musically while the different arrangements reflect the lyrics. Eventually, our expectations are met as we realize what they are doing.

This might sound complex, but as a songwriter you have to learn to listen to songs this way. You can still enjoy your favorite songs, but at times you have to listen to them analytically to understand what master songwriters are doing to make their songs sound so good to you. How does the melody reflect the words? How does the harmony set the mood for the song? What expectations do you have as a listener, and how soon are these met? How does the chorus differ from the verses, and how is it set up? These general approaches are important; you can learn them without plagiarizing.

Listen to all sorts of music and become familiar with even those genres that don't appeal to you right now. First, you never know what you may come to like through more exposure. Then you have to be sure that you don't think you are coming up with something new while inadvertently copying an existing style. You might also get ideas you can incorporate into your own style. Maybe most importantly, your audience may be listening to them, too.

While songwriting can seem like a solo pursuit, you have to consider your listeners. At some point you will want to share your music with at least a few people, and you want to be able to communicate with them. While your song may be well-crafted, you still don't want to sound like a second-rate version of another artist, and you won't be able to do something original until you know what's already been done, and what your audience *knows* has been done. You are expanding your horizons so you can expand theirs as well. (It's bad enough sounding like a warmed-over version of a current pop star, but it's worse being the only person present who doesn't know!)

You have to learn to trust your ear, but you can trust it only when it becomes *educated*. This means knowing the basics, knowing styles, knowing your audience, and knowing what you want to write. All of this takes time and practice. Music that is new or complex to you will take more time for you to understand, to "hear into it." The same is true of your audience. If you choose to write challenging music, remember that they will have to hear it a few times before they can judge for themselves. Once you realize how they have to work to understand your music, you will have a new respect for your listeners and a new tolerance and understanding of those whose music you are listening to.

But what are you doing when you "listen like a songwriter"? Let's look at analysis.

ANALYSIS

Every time we have looked at the lyrics, melody, or harmony of a song, we have done a little bit of analysis on it, so you are starting to get familiar with this process. Analyze other songs to learn what others have done and to get new ideas for your own songs. Analyze your own songs to improve them by applying what you have learned.

So what do you study in analysis? Pretty much anything in a song that is helpful to you. You can do the classical type of analysis that looks at how the melody fits with the chords. You can study the chord progression, look for chords from outside the key, or even a change of key. You can look at how the words fit with the melody, and how certain words – especially the title – are made to stand out. You can examine the rhyme scheme of the lyrics and relate it to the cadences, or just to the sections of the melody. But you do not need to limit yourself to this type of investigation.

Analysis is simply figuring out what is going on in the song. We want to know what the songwriter has done, especially those parts we find interesting. You may find a melody boring, but the words of a verse seem to fit it really well. It is worth figuring out how they work with the melody and how you can use that in your own song. Maybe the words avoid landing on a strong beat until they reach the most important word; that is certainly something worth knowing how to do. Maybe a song has a chord progression that fascinates you. More than just knowing what the chords are, you should find out why it is so interesting to you. In your analysis, what is interesting to you is what is important.

It is a good idea to keep a notebook or musical diary of these things, because quite often you will find that different things strike you when you are in different moods. Even the same event might sound different to you. For example, the end of "You Never Give Me Your Money" on the Beatles' *Abbey Road* album, when they start counting during the fade-out: This might sound sarcastic or ironic to you in a cynical mood, or perhaps hopeful in a more positive frame of mind. What causes that? Is it the descending bass of the progression that gives a "down" feeling to you, or maybe the final run up to the high A of the A major chord that gives you the uplift? The point is not to rip off the progression for your own song (most listeners will hear that immediately), but rather to learn about downward progressing bass motions and contradictory endings of phrases. What about it speaks to *you*?

Once your analysis uncovers something interesting, you are *almost half done*. Now work it into something that speaks for you. Don't say something someone else has already said, most likely better. To find your own voice, use the materials of music in your unique way. This can be slightly different from others or wildly original, but if it has already been done, it's been done. This is where you can develop your critical, discriminating ear.

As you analyze a song and begin to understand what the songwriter is doing, you will inevitably form opinions about it. Remember that you are learning about the song, not the writer. As anyone tries new things, they are liable to take dead ends or make big blunders. So give the songwriter the same respect and benefit of the doubt that you would want for your songs. And give yourself that benefit when analyzing your own songs! Remember this: "If you are not making mistakes, you are not trying anything new." A lot of our learning is trial and error, and the most valuable part can be so-called "error." It is hardly wrong if you learn from it. If you see it as a learning opportunity, you are miles ahead of those who just moan that they have "lost it" or are "no good." You have learned that something which seemed sensible does not work. Good! Now you can move on to something else. The more things you try, the more good ideas you will find. I'm not saying that you will not, or should not, be really disappointed when you try out a cool new idea that ends up sounding terrible. Be angry if you feel it. Sulk, get mad, blame your cat! Go wherever your disappointment takes you, but *don't stay there*. At the very least, you have learned something that doesn't work. The only truly wasted time is when you could be writing but aren't.

Most songwriters are influenced by other songwriters they admire. While it is good to take ideas from many different places, it is a terrible idea to blatantly copy someone else. Yes, there are copyright and legal penalties to worry about, but as a writer there is the bigger loss of your own voice and talent. A number of people have put it this way: "Stealing from one person is plagiarism; stealing from a hundred is influence." Stealing here is taking general ideas or approaches. Influences can be almost obvious and yet still sound fresh. The early Beatles played a lot of R&B and Motown songs as close to the record as they could manage, but they still maintained the "Mersey beat" that was at the core of their sound. They also wisely chose the B sides of the 45s – fillers that rarely got much airplay on radio and so were pretty much unknown. Finally, they played a large number of songs by "girl groups" of the time, sometimes not even changing the words to fit a male band, as in the song "Boys." The combination of influences was so compelling that the Beatles were able to bring American songs back to America and sound like something completely new; in the process, they generated huge royalties for several startled songwriters who thought their songs were long forgotten.

John Lennon and Paul McCartney wanted to be songwriters. They also wanted to play in a band. While they *gradually* learned the craft of songwriting, they played other people's songs as they learned from them and applied their own style to them. Even the most complex songwriters began simply; they became great by constantly improving. Playing other songs you love is still a great way to learn songwriting if you take the time and effort to learn what it is that makes you love them. You might even start by copying them if, like John and Paul, you are wise enough not to record or publish them. Better yet is to take a situation from a song you like and update it or personalize it. Say you like "In-a-Gadda-da-Vida": You might consider what a modern "garden of Eden" would be like, or what your personal version would be, and try to realize this in your lyrics, melody, and harmony.

Many songwriters pursue other arts and find that those perspectives are helpful in music as well. Painting seems to attract a lot of songwriters and composers, perhaps because the considerations of how colors look different depending upon the colors around them can be applied to musical harmonies. Also, the differences between juxtaposing primary colors versus gradually shading from one color to another create effects that can seem similar to how harmonic progressions work. "Color harmony" can teach a lot of subtle lessons on musical harmony, and analyzing the composition of a painting can lead to new insights when analyzing music. Any creative activity can affect your music.

Analyzing a draft of your own song means going through a version you have written to find things that don't quite satisfy you or things that you feel you could do better, and then improving them. It sounds simple, but often it's hard to change something you have written and grown attached to, even though you know it doesn't sound that good. The payoff is a final version that is much better than when you started.

Work on your song using all the material in the previous chapters. Once you have a good idea of what you want to say and how you want to say it, create a first draft. Then use the next chapter to analyze what you have so far. There you'll find an example of the stages of working through several drafts of a song until it is finished.

CHAPTER 9

A SAMPLE SONG DEVELOPMENT

Here's an example of how to take a simple idea and develop it into a song. In actuality, this is a hybrid of four real students' work and the issues we faced in our writing sessions (lessons). At this point, each of our budding songwriters had a short idea they liked and wanted to develop into their first song. Let's call our composite songwriter "Jake" and use Example 1 as his first idea. In this case, we have words, melody, and chords that Jake planned to play on his guitar to accompany his own singing.

Jake's first idea is shown below. It is typical of many beginners' first ideas. The final song, at least as far as we take it here, is not the best possible song from this idea; if you want to make your own changes as we work through this example, it will help you absorb the process. Just remember that you are working with a beginner's first attempt; it is constructed to show a number of changes that can and should be made. Be patient with Jake – in reality, you will be learning to be patient with yourself.

 Track 58

Example 1 – Jake's first idea

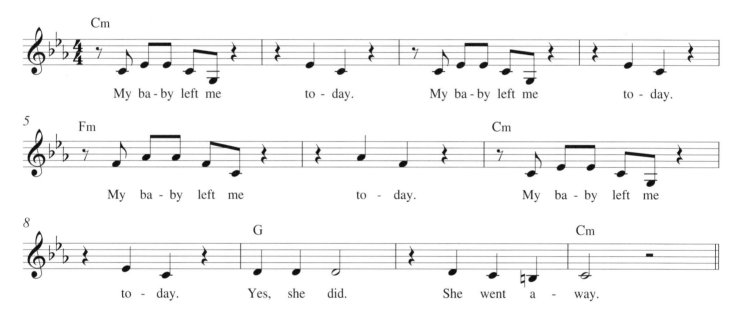

As a songwriter, one of the first skills you must develop is the ability to hear your own work with a naive listener's ears. No one knows, or cares, how much time you spent agonizing over your creation – they want to hear a song. Start by listening to the technical features. Specifically, do the words speak to most people or are they too personal to the writer? Does the melody flow and have direction or does it wander? Does it reflect the words, reaching its greatest point of tension or emotion when the words do? Does the song have a style?

We have now passed from a creative phase to a critical one. We have to think of it as someone else's song, as much as possible. Jake has got this much and likes it, so we critique it with an ear toward making it better, *not* toward trashing it. On reflection, Jake had to admit that it was overly repetitive in both words and melody. This is not the time to throw a song away, though, but to try our best to save it. The words are a good place to start, since lyric changes usually affect the melody.

In real life, Jake never referred to his significant other as "my baby," so it was fortunate that "my girlfriend" has the same number of syllables and the same pattern of accents. It also gets rid of a tired cliché and sounds more natural. "Today" set a time for her leaving, but "just now" has more immediacy; we can see the door closing and know we are hearing his immediate thoughts. It also fits the accent pattern of two quarter notes: "just *now*" has the strong accent on the strong beat.

When we reach the second phrase in bar 3, we understand the plot, so do we really need to repeat the lyric? It might seem vaguely "poetic," but lyrics aren't poetry. We want to tell a story in few words, one that people can understand on first hearing. They know she left you, but not how you feel about it. In this case, Jake's first feeling was that it was like the house was empty, although she was all that was gone. He wrote down some different lyrics:

My girlfriend left me, just now.
The house seems lonely, somehow.

After seeing the words, I was eager to hear Jake sing them, to see if he would avoid the "sing-song" effect that a literal repeat of two quarter notes can give when they rhyme like this. As I hoped, Jake added a syncopation that made the word "somehow" sound more natural by singing "how" just before beat 3 rather than right on it. He heard this when I asked him to play it slowly and listen to when he strummed the third beat; it came just after he sang the word. We changed the notation of bar 4 (see ex. 1a). Remember from the chapter on Rhythm that many singers add syncopation naturally, but in this case we have a syncopation that is important to keep the melody moving.

 Track 59

Example 1a – Syncopation of "somehow"

Now before we continue with the lyrics, let's think of where we are heading with our song. We need to consider telling our story and writing our melody at the same time, and we have options. We should consider as many of these as we can think of, rather than just what comes to us at first. This sort of knee-jerk writing can keep us in a rut, which is bad enough, but it can also lead to problems with plagiarism: We are likely to subconsciously continue along a line we have heard before but have half forgotten. These patterns often seem "natural" to our ears because we have heard them used successfully in the past, but we forget them. The section on copyright in the Melody chapter has more specific information, but at this point let's consider our options.

A good melody has one high point, which it builds to and then relaxes down from. Just as a well-written paragraph has a single strong point, our lyrics should have one idea or present one situation. Usually our emotional peak coincides with our melodic climax, although for special effect we might want them to conflict. However, since this is our first song, let's master the basics before we get fancy. A quick look over the melody shows that our melodic climax so far, the highest note, is on the word "baby." Even with the change to "girlfriend" this is not a word we want to build to or even emphasize first, since it is only the second word in the song. More importantly, the song is not about her – important as she is – but about Jake's reaction to her leaving.

At this point, Jake was only certain that her leaving was not what he wanted to be his main point in the first verse. It's easy to feel like you've hit a brick wall and obsess on what to do, and this can cause you to spin your wheels trying to find an answer that isn't there yet. This is the time to change gears and consider something else. In this case I asked Jake where the melody started to lag, to him as a listener. He felt that bar 4 was the spot: "I can hear it coming; I know before I get there what it will be."

So far, every bar has started with the melody resting on the first beat, so it made sense to start bar 4 on the first beat. To shape the melody we decided to extend it up to G, using the notes of the C minor chord as its basis. A quick switch of "working modes" moved us into creativity mode. After a few trials, Jake came up with a bar that fulfilled all our requirements and was something he liked. We now had given shape to the melody and added another motive in the triplet quarter notes on the downbeat. (See Example 2.) These might look complicated on the page, but they are the natural rhythm of the word "ev'rything" – just try saying it and you will hear the triplet feel "*one*-two-three." Then apply this same rhythm to "Empty somehow": "*one* -two-three- *one*."

Jake now wanted to reconsider both the rest of his lyrics and the melody for them. But before that, I felt it was important to look at the harmonic structure of the song. As we have seen, an eight-bar melody is a standard for almost all styles and yet this one is 11 bars; add another bar to turnaround via G7 to get back to the start and we have a 12-bar structure, which Jake correctly diagnosed as "bad blues, and not 'bad' in the 'good' sense." Following his instinct, Jake had inadvertently written a 12-bar blues, which also explained the repetitive structure of his melody. This is a classic crossroad that beginning songwriters face: Is your goal to write a blues, or have you fallen into the structure because you know it so well? In this case, Jake did not want to write blues, so it was time to rethink several aspects of the song.

First was the classic blues progression, which we looked at closely in the chapter on song forms. Consider where you might make changes to the progression that still support the melody. Bars 3 and 4 do fit Cm, but they also fit Cm/Ab (Abmaj7) and Cm/F (Fm9). Since Fm is coming up in bar 5, Cm/Ab was the more musical choice. This same process was applied by Jake at home when he had changed the lyrics to bar 6. The new words were "ev'rything's changed;" while the melody still fits Fm, it also fits Db. This was a great choice because it is unexpected, takes us even further from the standard blues progression and – most significantly – reflects the words so well. In fact, with the new lyrics, this gave a real punch to the melody's Ab, our highest note so far, and to which the first 6 bars build logically. Finally, it provides a fresh way to return to Cm in the next bar without it seeming obvious.

🔊 **Track 60**

Example 2 – Jake's first draft

The song's climax now comes in bar 9. On paper, this worried Jake because he had already used A♭ in bar 6 – and rather prominently at that – but when sung there is no doubt that we hear the climax in bar 9. This is because the A♭ of bar 6 was short and off the beat, as opposed to the longer, repeated one in bar 9 that is supported by the most dissonant chord so far: G7♭9. After this, we need to wind down to cadence on Cm in bar 11. While Jake was tempted to continue the G7♭9 into bar 10, it was much better to leave out the A♭ and simply play G7. A♭ has done its job well as a dissonant climax to a painful story, but it is more effective to let go of it in both the melody and the accompaniment. This lowers the tension and eases us into the cadence. The G7 of bar 12 leads us back to the start of the verse.

Look over the initial idea and the improved version, concentrating on the first eight bars. You want a balance of few enough musical ideas (or motives) for the melody to hang together, but not so few that it sounds repetitive and boring. When we first looked at this in the chapter on Melody, I said that it was not possible to give exact numbers in general. But this song is a great case study because the original had just two rhythmic ideas — the first in bar 1 and the second in bar 2 — while the improved version still has only three, but what a difference that one new one makes. The quarter-note triplet idea from bar 4 is repeated exactly in bar 8 and is varied in bar 6. This is enough to give the variety the melody needs without losing all sense of structure. Even the slight variation of the first rhythmic idea in bar 5, where the first eighth note is lengthened to a quarter note, still sounds right but gives a bit of variety, again using syncopation that follows the natural flow of the words.

Both versions use straight quarter notes for the last three bars of melody, which helps even out the movement into the cadence. The second version removes the rest on the first beat of bar 10 to enhance the smoothing effect; the only break in the quarter-note motion is the longer note on "she" that emphasizes the lost lover.

The lyrics are much improved by removing the repetition. We have more information on how the singer feels, but there are spots that could use more work, depending on how exacting you want to be. For example, would his immediate reaction be to sing about it when she has just left? It may sound a bit far-fetched, but Jake felt he would do just that. The song will always reflect the writer, so if you have taken your audience into account and decide to leave a lyric like this, it is your prerogative. Besides, he is singing a song. Just be sure you read for potential problem spots in this way.

This is clearly a man singing, which is fine if, like Jake, you are a guy who plans to sing his own songs. However, if you want others to cover your song, look for gender-neutral words that work for both. Here, you only need to come up with synonyms for "girlfriend" and "she," although that is often easier said than done. Otherwise, this can lead to an entire re-write of the verse. In this case, though, "lover" could work for male or female, and it fits the melody and accent structure. It would require just a rewording of the last line, which is not that strong anyway. Possibilities include "All because my love went away," and moving the half note to the beginning of bar 10, on the word "love." See Example 2a on page 74.

Example 2a – Alternate gender-neutral verse

THE CHORUS

So far I have referred to the idea as "the verse" because, in all four cases, we had aimed for a verse-chorus song. When you have refined your idea and are convinced you have it in good shape, consider whether it is a verse or the chorus. The 12-bar form rules out the 32-bar AABA standard form and the writers ruled out blues. Remember what we want in a chorus: a strong melody that can bear repeating, using the same words, and still sound fresh each time. Is it "catchy" enough to bear repeating several times unchanged? So far we have an emotion that everyone can understand – a loved one leaving them – but is there something unique about this that makes it stand out from all the other songs of lost love?

In general, a chorus should be short enough for the listener to keep in memory easily, usually eight bars often repeated (perhaps with some variation). If possible, it should be easy to sing so that your listeners can join in – and remember it better. Make the title prominent so that fans can remember its name. In our case with a 12-bar melody, it is a bit long for a chorus. Its melody is also not quite as memorable as we might like. It covers a wide range, but keeps returning to the lowest part of our singer's range. Finally, it sounds like a verse that is capable of supporting different lyrics.

As Jake went off to write a chorus, he needed to keep in mind that it had to be related to the verse but intensify the feeling by either going into it more deeply or finding a convincing contrast. A time-honored aphorism is that "life goes on and I will survive this stronger and wiser." One of our real-life Jakes went on a successful date and so naturally wrote this type of chorus with all the strength of belief. A move to a major key can give uplift to a song in minor; while we have seen that the relative major is the most closely related key, it would have been too smooth a transition for what needs to be a complete change in perspective, so we chose the parallel key of C major. This had the added benefit of making available our singer's highest note, the A♮ above the A♭ of the verse (a note missing from the relative major key of E♭), for a climax higher than the one in the verse. This also meant that the final G7 chord of the verse would lead into the chorus.

Example 3 – Jake's first draft of a chorus

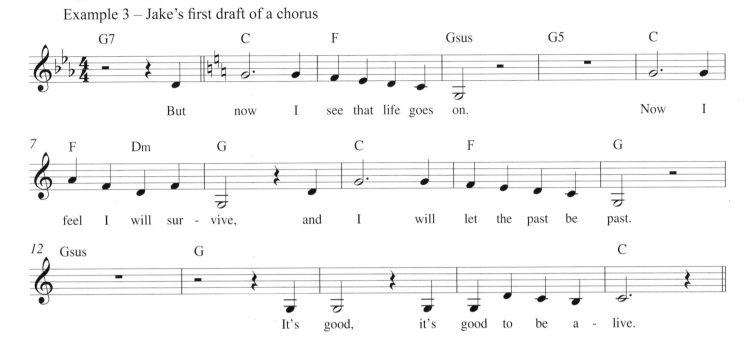

The first draft of the chorus (Example 3) uses only major chords (with one Dm) for the strong, positive tone they bring. The chorus gets off to a powerful start with the leap up to the G ("But now..."); the repeated "now" four bars later stresses that time has passed and his feelings have changed. (A nice parallel is that the uplifting chorus begins with a leap up a perfect 4th while many of the phrases in the verse ended by dropping a perfect 4th. That the writer didn't plan this makes no difference to its subconscious effectiveness.) The slight strain for the singer to reach the A on "feel" gives an emotional boost to the chorus. The third phrase repeats the first, but then the fourth drops to the lower range to relax into the cadence that will both set up the return to the verse, and later, the end of the song.

A pleasant lyrical touch was the echoes of "past be past" and "It's good," the second one having a nice spontaneous feel, as if he were adding this line on the spot. Subtle connections like these make the song hang together well without being obvious.

Once again, we switch from creative to critical mode. The first thing to notice is that the first three phrases end on the low G, and the fourth begins there. This note was prominent in the verse, and might get tiresome on repeated listening. Worse yet, the singer had trouble singing his own song with the leap down from F to G in bars 6 and 7, on the important statement that he will survive this terrible blow. (As he joked, "It sure doesn't sound like I survived. It sounds more like I leapt off a bridge!") We needed to change this phrase.

Humor is a great tool for critiquing without veering off into negative territory. The whole idea is to improve the work, and the focus should be on the improvements. Making light of the faults of the drafts reminds us that we are dealing with a draft and not a finished product – so the more improvements, the better.

As Jake accompanied himself on the guitar, a subtle harmonic point came up. His move from Gsus to G5 sounded "off." While this move would be fine in some styles, the most common progression would resolve the suspended 4th (the note C) to the 3rd of the chord, B. Instead, Jake was raising it to D, which still fit the chord but did not resolve the C. See Example 4 on page 76.

Track 63

Example 4

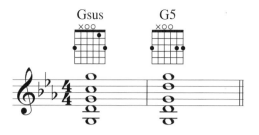

We refined the chorus in the session, ending up with Example 5, which contains our modifications and additions.

 Track 64

Example 5 – Jake's revised draft of the chorus

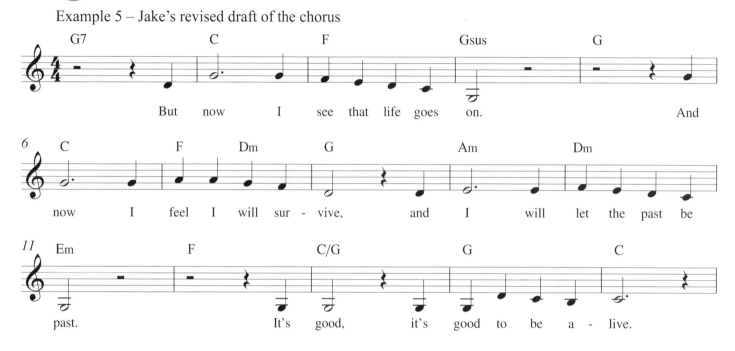

We kept the Gsus of bar 3 to give motion to bar 4 (life "going on"), where we resolved to G. The simple addition of "and" to this bar echoed the upbeat to the first bar of the chorus. The repeated G underplays the echo effect and increases the tension by starting in the upper register. The same idea fuels the repeated A in bar 5, lengthening the climax just that little extra bit, falling back to a D in bar 7 instead of the original G. With so much emphasis on G and A so far, bar 8 avoids a literal repeat of the first phrase by going up a step to E and only then walking down to the low G. This allows for more harmonic freedom. Having set the uplifting tone with the first two phrases predominantly in major, this is an opportunity to add a slightly more introspective viewpoint and use some minor chords.

The previous sections have presented suggestions and guidelines – not "rules." All excellent choruses speak (or rather, sing) for themselves, but there are general ideas you should keep in mind during critiquing sessions. One is whether you are aiming at an "anthemic" chorus: a fairly simple melody over a few major chords belted out by a strong voice backed by full band, choir, strings, and maybe even brass. Most people, can name several of their favorite songs that have this type of chorus, but at this point you are better off going for what is most persuasive for your song with consideration of your resources. This is the point of greatest diversity for my private students, and was especially true of the four I based this example on.

In the case of Example 5, the Am of bar 8 sounds fresh since it has not been used before, and also because it is a smooth "deceptive" cadence from the previous G (see Appendix D). This subtly signals a change in attitude, and provides the opportunity for a rising bass line (D-E-F-G) to contrast our descending melody, making a familiar phrase that much different. This adds an important dimension of movement (harmony *progressing*) to what had been a harmonically dead spot hanging on to G for four bars. C/G is similar to Gsus, but instead of just suspending the 4th over our bass G we also suspend the 6th, E. Rather than write Gsus4/sus6, C/G is simpler. It is also a strong progression for a cadence. (See Appendix E for more on the double suspension.)

Moving the last phrase down to the lower register relaxes the tension that began the chorus and cadences effectively on C. Beginning the phrase on G while the harmony is F may look odd on the page, but it anticipates the following G (see Appendix E for more on anticipations) and sounds good. At this phase it is a good idea, though, to experiment with changing it to a chord tone (F, A, or C) and judging the effect of each of these. Keeping in mind that the last note sung before this was a G, the G makes sense melodically. Beyond that, it enables the repetition of "It's good," which leads into a strong cadence and yet can sound as if it were being spontaneously discovered the first time through.

We have not yet chosen a title. A quick look over the lyrics of the chorus does not suggest any that stand out. Our options are to rewrite the lyrics of the chorus around a title we like, or to choose a phrase and perhaps work it more prominently into the lyric. Our four songwriters each had a different idea: one chose "It's Good"; another decided to use either "It's Good to Be Alive" or "It's Good (To Be Alive)"; the third chose the more poetic "But Now"; the fourth decided to wait and see if better lyrics came to him.

At this point, you can either repeat the process with your entire song or just the verse or chorus. This will depend on how satisfied you are with what you have and whether you feel you can improve it substantially. If you decide to go through it again, don't get caught in an endless loop of small changes. If you find yourself making miniscule changes or coming up with more alternatives, it is time to give it a rest. It is better to do this sooner rather than later, because too many changes can overload a song and make the next steps difficult. After one intense time through the song, Jake decided he liked what he had, so we moved on.

Having spent so much time on the details of fewer than 30 bars of music, it was time to put the song away for a few weeks and come back to it later with fresh ears. This is not easy because you will have been obsessing over the song for weeks or months. But you must get some distance from it, especially from the changes you have made. Put it in a drawer after you have made a good copy. Do not think you will remember "that last little bit" or "that obvious change." You won't.

If you are notating your song on a computer, put in every change and print it out with the date and time. If you are notating by hand, do a legible copy of the final version and again add the date and time. Then put it in a drawer (one where you will be able to find it again in a few weeks) and concentrate on your playing, or re-read parts of this book you needed for your song, or get back to bird-watching – whatever takes your mind off this song.

And do not play your song for anyone under any circumstances!

RETURNING TO THE DRAFT

It is important to put the song aside for a few weeks. I can usually tell who has sneaked a peek at their song – or even kept working on it – by their reaction to our return to the previous draft. In this case, the feeling among the four Jakes was an outburst ranging from "I'll never be a songwriter" to "everything I do is terrible" and worse. The positive side is that there is passion for this song and still strong discontent with its current state; you need that to continue improving it. In this instance, Jake realized his chorus does not lead back to his verse believably.

Think of it this way: We have reached our next challenge, and that's all it is – our next challenge. Look at what you have learned so far: We have a strong verse that gives a clear picture of what has happened and how it affects the singer. It's a feeling that most people know and can relate to. We have a strong chorus that adds variety while keeping to the same story and moving it along. We have good harmonic variety and nice arcs to our melodies. In a cooler frame of mind, we considered that life really does go back-and-forth, and after a serious breakup we might feel great one day, only to be back in the dumps the next. That is another thing most people can relate to, so use it. One of our real Jakes had an unexpected date that led us to an uplifting chorus, but it turned out they didn't hit it off and there was no second date. There is a good continuation for our story in the next verse: You will get through this, but it might take some time.

But before we get to that verse, we have to find a way to return from the chorus and its major key to the minor key – without a jolt. This is a problem with harmony, and is best solved that way. One option is to insert a short bridge passage with lyrics such as "but life doesn't always work out like that" or "things aren't always that simple." But since that will be the topic of the next verse, the least complicated means is to insert a short instrumental part to lead us back to the verse. We might use a guitar phrase as basic the one shown here. (The example is played twice on the audio track: first with straight-eighths, then with swing-eighths.)

🔊 **Track 65**

Example 6a – four-bar bridge passage

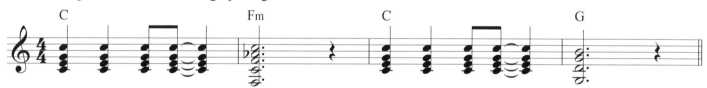

Here we introduce the minor mode with the Fm chord, but still in the key of C major. This softens the return to C minor. If four bars seems too short, expand it to eight, which also gives you the opportunity to introduce a Cm chord:

🔊 **Track 66**

Example 6b – eight-bar bridge passage

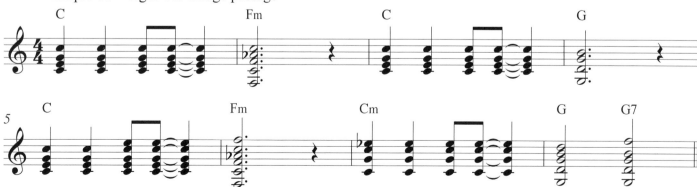

While the first choice gets you back to the verse quickly, the second matches the eight-bar units of the chorus. When you find that you have two seemingly good alternatives, it can be best to wait until the song is closer to finished before making the final choice. This will let you hear how each fits into the whole, and whether one is too abrupt or the other slows the pace.

As we return to the verse, another common problem appears. While writing and performing the verse alone, the songwriter has swung the eighth notes. (See the chapter on Rhythm for "swinging eighth notes.") The conflict was easily missed in the chorus because we use no eighth notes in it; by adding our bridge figure, the guitarist noticed he was playing these eighth notes straight but then singing the verse with swing. The simple solution is to play the bridge with swing, which affects only two notes, and continue into the verse. We might also choose to continue the swing accompaniment into the chorus, or play it straight for an even greater contrast. Our real-life Jakes split evenly between the two options; both have their merits. The important point is to find these spots that need improvement, to view them as challenges rather than as deficiencies in you as a songwriter, and to find a solution that pleases you and should please a listener as well.

Now that we are back to the verse, we can consider how many verses and choruses we might want. The first verse sets up the shock of the situation, and it would be abrupt to suddenly consider that "life goes on," which gives the impression that the relationship wasn't all that important anyway. A second verse would help clarify his feelings and set up the chorus more naturally. From there, it makes more sense to have the revelation of the chorus, followed by a "return to real life." Another chorus reaffirms the message that life does go on and gives us hope that our singer will not be jumping off a bridge any time soon. An ending could be as simple as repeating the last phrase to emphasize that he will be acting on his message.

An overview of the song and its story looks like this:

Verse 1: She left him, he's devastated, and everything has changed. (C minor)

Verse 2: Everything reminds him of her, his past has an aching gap, and life seems hopeless.

Chorus: Life goes on. He will get over it and life is good. (C major)

Verse 3: It won't be easy, getting over it. Sometimes he's up, sometimes down. Up is becoming more frequent. (C minor)

Chorus: Life goes on. He will get over it and life is good. (C major)

Coda: Repeats the last phrase, maybe a little slower.

Our next task is to write Verses 2 and 3. We know the general story we want to tell, and we know that our melody and accent structure should follow that of Verse 1. Extra syllables mean breaking longer notes into shorter ones, while sometimes the opposite is necessary to accommodate the lyrics. Remember that you are telling a story with some rhyme, not writing poetry. Most musicians find lyrics the most difficult part of songwriting, since they have spent so much time concentrating on playing melodies and harmony. Only singers will have devoted a lot of time to words and their accent patterns, and much of that is spent in others' songs and foreign languages. Don't be daunted by writing words. If you get stuck and start to get down on yourself, read over the lyrics of popular songs you like – don't sing, merely read them aloud. Most people come away from this exercise thinking "I can do at least as well as that!" And you can. Just tell your story and rhyme where necessary. If you can stay away from the most common rhymes like "moon/June," "love/dove," and so on then all the better.

Lyrics for the missing verses might be:

Verse 2
Can't believe that she's gone, no way.
I think of her smile, things she would say.
Ev'rything in here reminds me of her –
Stuff that was mine is now suddenly hers.
How did she take my life away?

Verse 3
It won't be easy, that much I know.
One day I'm okay, the next circuits blow.
Some days I believe I'm over it all –
The next day's a pit, and again in I fall.
It's my life, and I'm here to stay.

Obviously these words could use improvement, but they are just a first draft. The process begins again. While working with them you might find an idea that strengthens the melody of the verse, which then requires small changes in the other lyrics.

"WHEN AM I DONE?" – LEARNING TO FINISH A SONG

This may be the most important question of the whole book. Ultimately the answer is up to you, but my advice here is perhaps the most valuable I can give you.

Don't be a perfectionist

This trait probably kills off more would-be songwriters than any other. Perfectionists tend to have dozens, even hundreds, of unfinished songs that others would consider done, but the perfectionist can't stand the thought of not making each one "just a little better." You need to learn how to say "good enough." There will always be more to learn, better ways to say something you want to say, more effective melodies and chord progressions – but you have more songs to write and these are problems best addressed in your next song and the ones after that. They are what keep you writing! Realizing you are being a perfectionist is the first step in learning to finish a song. If this is deeply ingrained in you, try allowing this one song to be as it is. Make a deal with yourself to try it. You will have to make this deal again, but each time it will be easier.

Set a deadline

Even an artificial deadline can work wonders for creativity. This limits the amount of time you can waste wavering between two equally good alternatives and move you on to making changes that make a difference. Make your deadline realistic, but don't allow it to slip more than once. Be flexible in the case of true emergencies, but don't use small things as an excuse to let the deadline keep slipping because that will soon become your norm. You need to get a feeling for how quickly or slowly you work; this will become apparent over time as you write more and more.

Recognize diminishing returns

Keep your eyes and ears open enough to notice when your changes tend to be minor and have little effect on the sound of the song. Big changes are obvious and need to be made, but when your changes are between alternatives that are pretty much the same, you are spinning your wheels. You might want to start rationing your changes, say allowing five more changes and then "that's it." You are done. This often results in fewer than the five allowed.

Trust your gut

Most often you will feel that "it's done." This feeling becomes stronger over time, but you want to learn early in your writing career to differentiate between feeling that changes still have to be made and just being afraid to let go.

Put it away one last time

This time our goal is the opposite. We want to take it out of the drawer a few weeks later and realize we have done all we can at this point. Yes, in the future you will have more experience, more "tools" at your disposal, but this song reflects you now. If an important change seems obvious at this point, by all means fix it, but realize this is rare. Be sure it really is a significant alteration and it will not lead to a complete overhaul of the song.

SEND IT OUT INTO THE WORLD!

You know you are finished when you are confident playing it to a trusted friend or colleague, and when you know that, even if they do not like it, you do. Sure, rejection hurts, especially coming from a friend, but we waited until now to reveal the song to others for you to have enough belief in your song to know you did your best. You like what you have come up with.

Depending on your ambitions, share your song as you hope to continue. For most of us, playing our song for friends and family will be a rewarding experience in itself, and possibly as far as we want to take it. People have been doing this as far back as we know in history. If you are a performer, try out your first song on a friendly audience where your fans will be open to you branching out into songwriting. Gradually work up to more difficult crowds.

Listen to criticism, but do not take it to heart. Much criticism is thoughtless and not offered by experts. Remember that your critic is comparing you to the best songs of all time, a tough comparison to make for your first song! Let most of it go, but first be sure you learn what there is to be learned from the experience. Some will be humiliating, especially if you choose to perform your own material, but it can also be instructive. People are cruel enough to laugh at a song if they know it is your first attempt, but be careful to differentiate this from an audience that thinks they are laughing *with* you: This can show that something you meant as serious is coming across as comedic. If this keeps happening, you have a problem that needs correcting. This can be especially problematic with blues, as poorly written blues can come across as parody or satire.

Along the same line, if people keep talking through your verses but suddenly pay attention at the chorus, it shows you that your chorus is effective but you should see if you can intensify the verse in some way. This may be possible in the current song; if not, it is certainly a task for your next one.

Learn all you can from your critics, but then remember that you have crossed that magic threshold from zero to one songs written. You are a songwriter. Are they?

AND THEN?

Print a final copy and celebrate. You might want to frame it and keep it on the wall in your music room – or make it the background image for your computer or Facebook page or website. Remind yourself that it is done and you *are* a songwriter.

Then start song number two.

CHAPTER 10
WHAT NEXT?

Take a moment and bask in the realization that you are a songwriter. Now that you have created a song, you know you can do it. You have proof.

From here, you will improve your ability. Don't wait too long to start your second song. Remember all those hard decisions where you had to leave out a great idea because it didn't fit your first song? They can be the start of the second! Or maybe you couldn't decide whether the song should be fast or slow; if so, use the other tempo and vary your first song to fit it. If it's a fast one in major, try a slow minor version of it. Branch out slowly into new areas of form, harmony, lyrics, whatever interests you the most. Try chords outside the key. Play around with 7th chords. Try the jazz ii-V-I progression in all types of songs. If your first song was slow, speed it up and see how it sounds. You may have heard that the Beatles' No. 1 hit, the rockin' "Please Please Me," started out as a slow Roy Orbison type their producer George Martin insisted they try to speed up. Keep gathering ideas for lyrics in a notebook and melodies in recordings. Even the smallest idea can spark a whole song at the right time, when you are in the mood. Continue to beware of breaching copyright, a serious business that can stop your career before it starts – and cost you your house! Now that you have a song, you can understand why others are so protective of their work. Be respectful of that, and don't copy.

Along with your increase in technical knowledge, develop a tolerance for criticism, because the more successful you are and the wider your music is known, the more criticism you will attract. That is the flip-side of success. When viewed that way, it is a good thing: You are getting a solid reaction. Strong feelings can flip from hate to love, but weak indifference rarely changes. The music business has a harsh side you must learn to endure if you wish to make it a career. From the songwriting perspective, this becomes much easier when you know your work is good, and you can see your critics' words for what they are: opinions, and often ill-informed ones at that, even from loved ones.

Luck or chance plays a large part in the success of a song, just as with numerous things in life. So many factors influence the reception of music that the inherent excellence of a song is often lost in its consideration. Incredible as it seems, "Over the Rainbow" was originally cut from *The Wizard of Oz* because its slow tempo was felt to stop the dramatic momentum of the show. It took months of sustained effort by composer Harold Arlen and lyricist Yip Harburg – who were already famous – to rally enough support to get it reinstated. Not only did the song win the Academy Award for Best Song that year, it was later voted the greatest movie song of all time by the American Film Institute. Sometimes even you as the songwriter might be your worst enemy. As he admits, Keith Richards fought tooth and nail to keep his song "(I Can't Get No) Satisfaction" from being released as a single, thinking it was too basic and that the fuzz box was too much of a gimmick.

Helping someone else is the fastest way to improve. Seeing others struggle with the same problems you had, or are having, will help you realize it is not "you," but the challenge of songwriting. We all have days when every lyric we come up with sounds inane, or no melody seems to fit some great words. If you can, work through these problems. This can become a fine balance. You do not want to give up as soon as you hit a challenge; it is often a good idea to keep working at something until the solution finally hits you. However, you don't want to keep banging your head against the wall because you just can't get something that works. You have to learn about yourself, and gradually develop a working method that fits the way you work and the time you have to devote to songwriting. The ideal is to do a little every day rather than hours on one day a month. This type of scheduling is difficult in our complicated society, but it is much like learning an instrument. Taking a workshop or joining a songwriting group can help, too.

TEACHERS

No book can take the place of a qualified teacher, although my hope is that this one will help you complete that all-important first song. Many people find the confidence to approach a teacher only when they have one or two songs finished that they like. This is reasonable; you don't want to waste your money and time if you think songwriting is not for you. When you do decide to look for a teacher, don't just start with the first one you find. You need to consider how the person teaches and whether you can form personal rapport with them. It doesn't matter if the person has written dozens of Grammy-winning songs; if you don't connect with them, you won't get to that level. First see how interested they are in *your* music. Lots of teachers want to teach, but not as many are interested in the products of their students. You need a teacher who is committed to making you a better songwriter. In fact, if you are really good, you need a teacher who is okay with you being a better songwriter than they are. Lots of people say it, but not all mean it.

Psychologists who study learning have found two basic types of teacher-student relationships: master-apprentice and mentor-friend. While there are grey areas between the extremes, a teacher tends to be a master or a mentor, which forces the student into becoming either an apprentice or a friend. I'll go into these in some detail because confusion can be disastrous. Years ago I had the privilege to study with a famous virtuoso and brilliant musician. He was an outgoing but gruff kind of person who had a heart of gold and really cared about teaching. Unfortunately, he was a "master" type while I tried to be a "friend;" the results were a mess. Whenever I had an idea it would be "try my way first and then maybe we'll look at yours." Of course, we never looked at any of mine. I was blind to the mismatch, but finally had to quit my lessons; it was years before I had any idea of what had gone wrong. That's a lot of wasted time, work, and money.

You might want a master teacher if they are someone who writes just the kind of song you love and the type you would like to emulate, maybe with a slightly different spin. If so, it makes sense to master that style; after you have it completely under your belt, try branching out slightly, although at this point your teacher may get upset and you may have to look for another. Still, a master is the type of teacher for someone who thrives on being told "do this" and then doing it and getting good results. Many musical traditions have used the apprentice model, including jazz, blues, rock, and classical. This is the dominant model of university and college teaching, but teachers vary.

The mentor-type teacher tends to be more flexible, offering ideas to explore rather than methods to copy. A mentor I once had suggested I write a whole song using just one chord, which gave me a new appreciation for harmony. (When I brought back a pretty inane song and suggested that no one would really do that, he played me "Whole Lotta Love.") Similarly, there was an exercise to write a song without a melody, using just one note. That seemed impossible, although it expanded my harmonic vocabulary enormously. He played "One Note Samba" and the beginning of "Lucy in the Sky with Diamonds" to show me how others had tried the same experiment. I am the kind of person who likes puzzles and challenges, so this teacher was perfect for me. Some colleagues who studied with master teachers progressed faster than me at first, with instructions such as writing a song using all ii-V-I progressions and having them critiqued for "authenticity to the genre," but after a few years it evened out. You can't go on imitating someone else forever; at some point, you have to learn the basics of your craft in as many styles as you can. Both types of teacher will get you to the destination if they are good teachers, but you are more likely to give up if you don't have a good match of your learning style with their teaching style.

Be careful of teachers who want you to write like they do, following their exact method. Beware of teachers who spend more time on their songs than yours. Watch out for those who talk in vague generalities about what is wrong with your song, rather than demonstrate how to improve it. I consider it a good lesson when there is more music than talking, and more of the student's music than my criticisms. Examples of criticisms that I use: "Can you think of a richer-sounding chord for bar 2?" "How did that sound to you? Better than the first version or not? Why?"

But that's me. You are well on the way to finding your own style in songwriting, and that will extend to finding the teacher who is right for you. Keep writing with an open mind and you will improve.

I wish you success, but more importantly I wish you the enjoyment and satisfaction that writing music can bring.

"I DON'T WANT TO LEARN THEORY!"

Whenever I teach songwriting or an instrument, an inevitable question is "Will I have to learn theory for this?" At least that's the politest way of putting it. It ranges from "I'd rather not learn theory" to "The first whiff of theory and I'm outta here!" Before I got a serious complex about it, I began to realize that what most musicians are concerned about is their idea of what "theory" is. I used to get by teaching "how music works" and having my students be happy with that, but I later realized it was more of a service to them to discuss what theory actually is, and – more importantly – what it is not.

Theory is not rules. Theory is not marked exams. Theory is not textbooks or exercises or quizzes or all the similar stuff used to throw information at a student and hope some of it sticks. It would be better to replace the word "theory" with "facts," except that this would be misleading, too. And since it has been used for so long, we are stuck with the word.

Theory is our best estimate of how music works and how it has worked best for people in the past. It is always evolving, but there is a core that stays constant so that we can communicate with one another. Communication is the operative concept. Again, it might be a better word than theory, except now "communication" is a word that has its own problems. We are still left with theory. But theory allows important musical communication. Say your rehearsal breaks down and you tell the guitarist "In bar 45, that's an Am chord; you played D. Let's start again from three bars after letter B." The entire band needs to know about bars, how to count them, what rehearsal letters mean, what chords are, what the two mentioned are. The guitarist needs to know the Am chord he should play.

Much of music theory is like English grammar, except that it works for people who speak many different languages. You need to know the alphabet in which you write, then you need to be able to form words and know what they mean, and finally you need to be able to write sentences. If you want to write more than the occasional postcard, you need to learn to write paragraphs or longer essays, and how to express what you want to say. It helps to know about things like nouns and verbs, especially if you are going to get guidance or criticism for your writing.

Read this sample paragraph and think of suggestions you might give a friend on how to improve it – without using "technical" terms like noun, verb, subject, or object, all that "theoretical stuff":

> Got a Wes Montgomery DVD. Played lousy but so good. Fingers bleeding need bandages? They play such a. And Wes had that word, you know, for being good with his fingers. Coffee with a little sugar.

We need to know a lot: First, what was lousy and what was so good? Without subjects in the sentences we don't know if the writer is saying that Wes played lousy, or the DVD, or maybe the writer trying to play along. The same with "so good" – who is the subject here? Without a verb, the part about fingers bleeding makes no sense: maybe a shopping list? Or is it saying that Wes played so hard his fingers were bleeding? Or again, the writer? It's also hard to praise someone when you don't know the adjective that means he's "good with his fingers." Finally, what does the last sentence have to do with anything?

It's hard enough to write original thoughts when you know the basics of sentence formation, but without it, such writing is impossible. While the reader needs to be able to recognize the structure of sentences, the writer needs to be able to construct them, specifically as they relate to the thoughts to be written, and then to present them in a logical sequence.

So for our music theory, we want something similar to grammar that teaches us how to communicate clearly with other musicians. That is the basic level of musical literacy. We need to be even more conscious of the effect of our communication if we want to be a creative writer – a songwriter. Then we need to shape our communication to get across specific ideas in our own way. As an individual starting out, we cannot expect to change the way our audience hears music. They have heard a lot of it before and each one has their own pre-conceptions, so we need to work with what they already know. If we are good at it, we might be able to change their perception slightly toward what we consider our own style. We cannot come up with something new unless we know what has already been done.

Imagine a scientific genius who takes a few basic science courses and spends the rest of his life creating his Theory of Relativity, only to discover on his deathbed that Einstein did it over 100 years ago! If only he had known, what real discoveries might he have made? The same is true of a musician who knows only the barest theory and recreates Beethoven's Fifth Symphony or Gershwin's "Summertime" or the Beatles' "Sgt. Pepper's Lonely Hearts Club Band."

Some people claim you can pick up theory on your own, and much of it you can. But it takes a lot of time, and that time is better spent writing songs than trying to figure out which version of 9th chords makes more sense. This is an example of a sort of hair-splitting in which two "rival" theories present the same information, but interpret it in two different ways, when it is the information that is important.

For example, many classically oriented instructors teach major and minor scales and the diatonic chords as the basis of music. Other chords are then considered "advanced harmony." This advanced harmony is taught in conjunction with the historical periods that used the more advanced chords. On the other hand, jazz presents 7th chords as the norm and other chords as logical extension of "stacks of 3rds." Jazz teachers often concentrate on scales and modes that are harmonized by these chords with an emphasis on their use in improvisation – an art that has disappeared from most classical teaching. Over time, the material taught by each group tends to converge so that the same ideas are taught from different perspectives. As songwriters, we can have the best of both worlds by understanding both the material and the different perspectives. After all, serious classical composers such as Ravel and Copland have incorporated jazz into their compositions, while songwriters such as Gershwin and McCartney have used their knowledge of jazz, blues, and rock to create classical compositions.

Businesses are now in the thrall of "big data," where they collect the habits of millions of people through social networking and are able to spot trends and use these to sell gadgets and services. The idea is nothing new to music theorists, who have been using a version of "little data" to determine what works in the songs of the great songwriters, and incorporate that information into our current theory. In the later 20th century, we started to see a split between "classical music theory" and a more useful version of theory that applied to the music of the current day – which was pretty much what music theory had been in the Classical Era, ironically. Based on the success of jazz theory as a valid perspective, "popular music theory" extended the idea to a theory of other mainstream music. So while classical theory criticized the V7-IV7 progression as "primitive" or just "wrong," broader-minded theorists (jazz and popular) realized that this was a basis of the blues that provided its unique character and made it attractive to its audience. Similarly, the progression from I to ♭III in a major scale was virtually unheard of in classical theory because the major III chord (F in the key of D) uses the minor 3rd instead of the major 3rd that is part of the key; it also lowers the leading tone (F♯) to F♮. This progression became a staple of rock music, showing up in "Sgt. Pepper's Lonely Hearts Club Band" and "Smoke on the Water," to name just two classic rock songs. The validation of songs with simpler chords, often just major and minor, became part of popular music theory, which obviously has deep connections with both classical and jazz.

Theory is a delicate blend of what has worked in the past combined with new innovations. Various harmonic movements using "power chords" by half step or tritone have become common over the past decades. While they are now accepted into our vocabulary, we don't know if they will remain a vital force or end up sounding either dated or classic in years to come. The important thing is that they are not rejected out of hand because "that's not the way music is written." It is songwriters and other composers who determine what theory is based on, not the other way around. I suggest you consider theory to be anything that helps you write better. You can learn a lot from almost any style of music or any version of music theory, but don't let these weigh you down. As your style evolves you will find more things useful, but you will also run across ideas that don't help. Let those go for the time being. Concentrate on writing the better song you are aiming for.

INTERVALS AND SCALES

A musical interval is the distance between two notes, either horizontally (melodically) or vertically (harmonically). Intervals are identified by number, such as 2nd, 3rd, 4th, etc. and a modifier like major, minor, perfect, and so on.

Track 67

The number part of an interval is easy to find: just count the letter names, including the one you start on and the one you end on. Thus, A to C is a 3rd, which we count A-B-C. From F up to B is a 4th: F-G-A-B.

Track 68

For this short tutorial we will consider only intervals up to an octave, which is where the letter names start to repeat; e.g., A to A is an octave, as is C to C, and so on. The intervals above an octave merely add 7 (so G to A is a second; if that A is an octave higher it is a 9th, but it just sounds like a 2nd an octave higher).

Track 69

Within the octave, there are two divisions of intervals: some have major and minor forms (larger and smaller versions of the same number name), while others have only one form and are called "perfect." The intervals with major and minor versions are 2nd, 3rd, 6th, and 7th; perfect intervals are unison, 4th, 5th, and octave.

The smallest interval used in our Western music is a minor 2nd (half step). On the piano, this is the nearest key, black or white; on a guitar it is the next fret. Without taking a full course in theory, one way to tell the difference between a major and a minor interval is to count the number of minor 2nds contained in the interval. For example, a minor 3rd is made up of three minor 2nds, while a major 3rd has four. A minor 2nd is also called a half step or semitone. These terms can be used interchangeably. You might read that a perfect 5th is seven half steps or seven semitones. They mean the same thing; in fact, it is more common to use one of these terms rather than minor 2nds in situations where that might be confusing.

When studying music theory, one of the first things a student learns is all the major scales, including their key signatures. One of the advantages of starting with the major scale is that the intervals of each note from the tonic note will be either major or perfect. So in the key of C, C to D is a major 2nd, C to E is a major 3rd, C to F is a perfect 4th, C to G is a perfect 5th, C to A is a major 6th, C to B is a major 7th, and C to the higher C is a perfect octave. To find any of the minor intervals, just lower the upper note of a major interval with a flat or a natural.

In the C major scale above, P1 means perfect unison, M2 means major 2nd, and so on. (For a minor second, we use m2.) If the idea of a perfect unison looks odd with the scale, just think of two people singing or playing the same note.

If we want to make any or all of the major intervals into minor intervals, we lower the note by a half step using a flat (or a natural for a sharp note).

Notice that we did not change the perfect intervals. If you look back at the previous example, you will see a problem with lowering a perfect interval. Lowering C by a half step gives us the note B. Similarly, lowering F gives us E. The only perfect interval note we can lower without duplicating a note in the major scale is the perfect 5th. This is a special case in many ways. It is the dominant note of the key, so lowering it removes the dominant. It is also a popular note in blues and jazz, for reasons that turn out to be similar.

DIMINISHED AND AUGMENTED INTERVALS

As we saw, it is possible to lower the perfect 5th and get a new note that is not in the scale. It is possible to lower any perfect interval, in which case we call it "diminished." Thus a perfect 5th lowered a half step is a "diminished 5th." A perfect 5th raised a half step is an "augmented 5th." The same applies to a unison, 4th, and octave.

Major and minor intervals can also be made into diminished and augmented ones. Lowering a minor interval makes it diminished, while raising a major one makes it augmented. It can help to think of *minor* as "the smaller of two possibilities" and *major* as "the greater of two possibilities." Augmented means "made larger" and diminished means "made smaller."

INVERSIONS

We usually think of intervals counting up from the bottom note, say from C up to A (a M6). If we take that bottom note and put it up on top (becoming in our example A up to C), we end up with the inversion of the interval (a m3). A quick way to figure out inversions is to subtract the original number from 9 (e.g., 9 − 6 = 3) and to change a minor interval to major, or as in our example, a major interval to minor. Perfect intervals stay perfect, so that a perfect 5th inverts to a perfect 4th, and vice versa.

KEYS AND KEY SIGNATURES

Every major key has a different key signature, an arrangement of sharps and flats shown at the start of a song that stays in effect for the whole song (unless it changes key.) Each key needs its own key signature so that this same pattern of intervals is kept for every major scale; the relationships between the notes (and their positions in the scale) are kept the same, even though the names of the notes change. Every major scale follows the same pattern of whole steps (two half steps) and half steps. Using W for whole steps and H for half steps, the major scale pattern is W-W-H-W-W-W-H. This means that if D and G♯ are the second notes of their respective major scales, they will always be a major 2nd from their own tonic note (D from its tonic C; G♯ from its tonic F♯).

Let's check that pattern with the C major scale:

Track 72

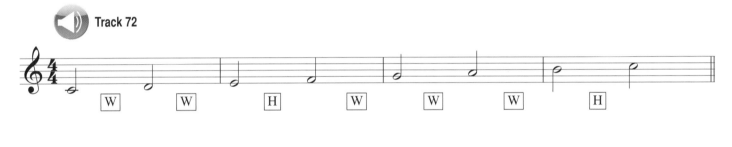

Now let's look at the G major scale. Without a key signature, it does not have the right pattern of W and H to form a major scale:

Track 73

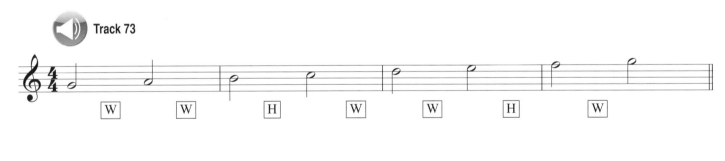

We need to fix the last two notes. Raising F to F♯ solves both problems:

Track 74

Notice that G is a perfect 5th above C. Adding one more sharp gives us the key of D major, which is a perfect 5th above G. The sharp we add is C♯, the leading tone to D.

Track 75

Each major key signature adds one more sharp to the preceding one. The sharp is always necessary to create a leading tone. The pattern of *ascending* to the next higher key by adding a sharp to create a leading tone creates the Circle of 5ths, which is covered in detail in most harmony books. The pattern with sharps looks like this: C-G-D-A-E-F♯-C♯. When we reach C♯, all notes are sharp so we can go no further.

What about flats? To get flat keys, we add one flat at a time to get keys that *descend* a perfect 5th. So the key of F, a perfect 5th below C, has one flat:

Track 76

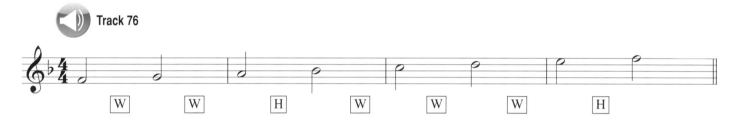

The leading tone E was already a half step below the tonic F. Our one flat (B♭) was necessary to maintain the W-W-H-W-W-W-H pattern of the major scale. Every flat added is on the 4th degree (IV) of the new scale. The pattern of flat keys is: C-F-B♭-E♭-A♭-D♭-G♭-C♭. When we reach C♭, all notes are flat and we can go no further.

G♭ is the same note as F♯, but spelled differently. Such notes are called *enharmonic*. The notes in both of their keys sound the same, and this is the point where the system overlaps. C♭ is enharmonic with B, both as a note and a key, but most writers prefer B with five sharps, rather than C♭ with seven flats. The whole system of keys is: C-G-D-A-E-B-F♯/G♭-D♭-A♭-E♭-B♭-F-C. Theory texts usually show this as a circle, with C at the top and F♯/G♭ at the bottom, thus the Circle of 5ths. (See below.) This is not crucial information for a songwriter, but it is helpful in remembering the number of sharps or flats in any key.

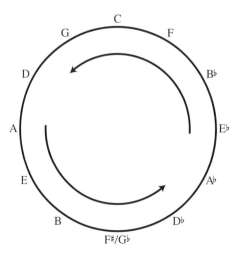

TRIADIC HARMONY

Harmony is the sounding of two or more notes at the same time. Our system of harmony is built on the idea of three-note chords called "triads" (tri = 3, as in triangle, tricycle, etc.). Music theorists name the chords in a key by the number of the placement of their root in the scale of the key. For example, the triad built on the first note of the scale is I, the one on the fourth note of the scale is IV, on the fifth note is V, and so on. We use Roman numerals to name triads. Uppercase numerals are for major chords: I, II, III, IV, V, VI, and VII; lowercase are for minor chords: i, ii, iii, iv, v, vi, and vii. We use uppercase for augmented chords and lowercase for diminished chords as well, since these are relatively rare compared to major and minor chords. (As with major and minor chords, uppercase denotes chords with a major 3rd, lowercase denotes a minor 3rd.)

MAJOR KEYS

The example below demonstrates the three major triads in the key of C, as well as the notes of the scale they harmonize. The notes C and G can be harmonized by two different chords: both F and C triads contain the note C, while C and G contain G.

🔊 Track 77

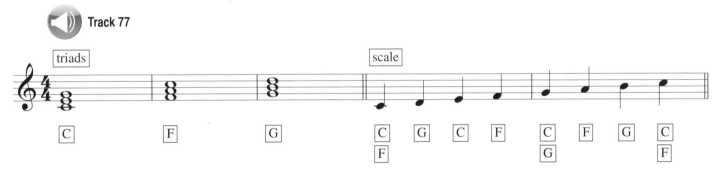

Just three triads can harmonize every note in our C major scale; this is true of every major and minor scale. So if you write a melody in the key of C, you need to know only the chords C, F, and G (I, IV, and V) to harmonize any note.

You can also see another reason why the number 3 is so important to our system: the notes of each triad are three notes apart in the scale. So the I chord – C major – consists of C, E, and G (**C-D-E**) and (**E-F-G**). The lower notes are a major 3rd (four half steps) apart: C-E, F-A, and G-B. The upper 3rd is a minor one: E-G, A-C, and B-D. This arrangement creates a major chord. (Minor chords reverse this order, with the minor 3rd below the major 3rd.) Another way of looking at the same notes is that the bottom note is the root of the chord (the note it is named after), the middle is the 3rd above the root, and the top is the 5th above the root; thus we have a chord made up of a root, 3rd, and 5th.

Many songs use just the three major chords of a major key. They form the basis of blues and rock 'n' roll, as well as many other styles. In general terms, the IV chord moves away from the home key and the V chord moves back toward it. The I chord is the main chord of the key, defining the tonality and so is called the *tonic* chord. Many songs begin with the tonic chord, and virtually all songs end on the tonic. (Some writers get around this by having a song fade out, but save this until you are comfortable writing final cadences.)

In the chapter on Melody, we saw how important it is to give the singer a chance to catch their breath. We break our melodies into phrases that usually end with a cadence. Harmonically, cadences typically end on the I or the V chord. Full cadences end on the I chord and have a final sound to them, much like a period at the end of a sentence. We customarily end large sections with a full cadence, most often the verse and the chorus. A half cadence ends on the V chord, and is more like a comma where we take a slight pause and continue. Like commas, these occur more often in the middle of sentences when we want a short break. Full cadences are generally V-I because the movement of a 5th from G down to C is strong, and the leading tone resolves up to the tonic note. A much softer, less common ending cadence is the IV-I "Amen" cadence. The half cadence can move either I-V or IV-V. (See Appendix D for more detail on cadences.)

If only three chords are needed to harmonize a key, why would we use more? Variety. While we don't need to use the other chords, they can spice up our melody by giving it a different background or even suggest different melodic directions. We can build a triad on every note of the scale. Here are the triads in the key of C:

Track 78

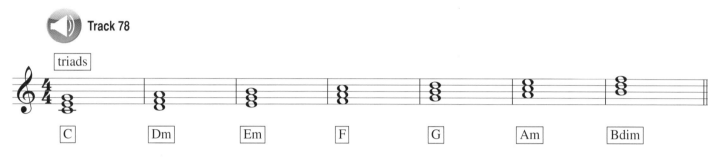

The new triads are minor chords on ii, iii, and vi as well as a diminished chord on vii. Remember that we use lower-case Roman numerals for minor and diminished chords. Each minor triad shares two of its notes with one of the major chords, and can be used as a substitute for that chord.

Track 79

The A minor chord (vi) shares C and E with C major (I), and can be used in its place anywhere except as the final chord of a song. D minor (ii) shares F and A with F (IV) major and is a good substitute for it. E minor (iii) is a bit less useful as it shares G and B with G major (V), but also E and G with C major (I); it contains the leading tone, but does not move strongly to the tonic chord. This can lead to some beautiful chord progressions, but the iii chord in a major key does not work well as a general substitute for V, especially in a cadence.

The diminished chord on vii has a particular sound due to its diminished 5th from the root. It can also be considered a stack of two minor 3rds. Classical music regularly avoids it, or adds a 3rd below it, making it into a V7. Jazz and some popular music add a 7th to it, which works well. (See the next section.)

MINOR KEYS

Traditional conservatory harmony is often at its worst in teaching minor keys. The problem is a strict adherence to the harmonic minor scale, which gives a set of chords that are almost never found in real music. Jazz often takes advantage of the ii chord (Bdim in the example below), but adds the 7th above it making it a ii7♭5 (sometimes called a half-diminished 7th chord). The augmented chord is rare. In fact, leaving it as a major chord gives us the tonic chord of the relative major key, so that the ii chord contains the leading tone of the relative major; these two make it easy to transition, or modulate, from minor to relative major and back.

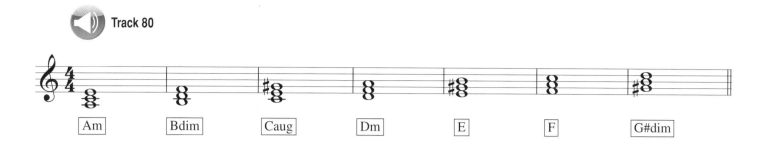

Similar to the diminished triad's diminished 5th, the augmented triad's particular sound comes from its augmented 5th. It can also be considered a stack of two major 3rds. Like the diminished triad, this use of the same interval in both positions gives the chord an unsettled sound. The diminished triad is like a minor chord with a lowered 5th, while the augmented chord is like a major triad with the 5th raised. Regardless of theory, if these chords spark your imagination, use them.

7th CHORDS

If we consider triads as stacks of 3rds, we can understand the concept of extending the stack to include more and more notes. Since a triad contains a root, 3rd, and 5th, the new notes we add should then be a 7th, 9th, 11th, and 13th. We stop at 13 because a 15th is a double octave (two octaves above the root) and the whole thing just starts over again. This uses all the notes in the scale, but we use only odd numbers to form chords. These odd-numbered chords are most often extended versions of the dominant 7th chord. If we need to omit any notes to make them fit, we need to keep the 3rd and the 7th because these form the tritone that signals the dominant 7th function (major chord with major 3rd and minor 7th).

Classical music theory considers 7th chords advanced, with rules about handling them (e.g., the need for all 7ths to resolve downward). Jazz theory considers 7th chords the norm, even for the tonic. They can add sophistication to your progressions if that is what you are looking for, but there is one that you need to know about regardless of your style: the dominant 7th, or more simply V7. Looking at the other types of 7th chords will reveal why V7 is important enough to cross genres.

Major chords usually take a major 7th and become major 7th chords, and minor chords use minor 7ths to become minor 7ths. Diminished chords take either a minor or diminished 7th. (Diminished chords with a diminished 7th form a stack of all minor 3rds, which gives the chords a spooky, horror movie effect.) The V chord is important because it is a major chord that has a minor 7th on top. This creates a V7, a powerful chord because it has three *tendency tones* that need resolution.

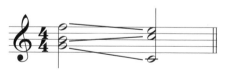

Not only does the root fall a 5th and the leading tone rise to the tonic, but now the 7th falls to the 3rd of the tonic chord. This is the strongest cadence we have: V7-I.

It is important for you to know the major, minor, and dominant 7th chords (e.g., A, Am, and A7). It's also useful to know the major and minor 7th version of chords. (See the following example.)

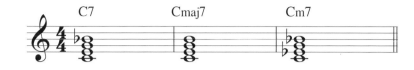

Track 82

After these, instead of learning all the other types of chords, you can try changing bass notes under major and minor chords. For example, the bass F sounds great under an Am chord – spelled Am/F. The sound is the same whether you spell it Am/F or Fmaj7; if Am works with the melody, so will Am/F. Similarly, A/B is the same chord as B11. If you are looking for new sonorities to inspire you, take chords you already know and just add a new bass note to them. You will find some great sounds experimenting this way.

If you have been taught harmony as a series of rules, now is the time to gently let them go. In songwriting there are no rules, so think of what you have learned as *expectations*. Much traditional harmony teaching is based on the idea that you must follow a simplified version of what Bach, Haydn, Mozart, and Beethoven did. In actual fact, however, there was never a time that people wrote harmony the conservatory way. So when we say, for example, that the leading tone resolves to the tonic or that V7 resolves to I, we are saying we expect these resolutions. You, as the songwriter, can choose to confirm our expectations or to startle us and do something different. A few surprises are good for a song and keep it from being clichéd, but too many will frustrate our sense of expectation and make your audience think you don't know "how to write music." This is one of the tricky balances that a songwriter has to learn, and it varies with genres and styles.

9th CHORDS

Adding one more 3rd to a 7th chord stack gives us a 9th chord. The 9th chord is identified by the presence of a 3rd and a 7th in the chord, in addition to the 9th. Simply adding a 9th to a triad, as say adding a D to a C major chord, is usually called an "add 2" chord, the 9th being the same note as the 2nd, just an octave higher.

Adding a 9th to a dominant 7th chord creates a dominant 9th, usually just called a 9th, as in D9 or C9. Adding a major 9th to a major 7th creates a major 9th chord (e.g., Cmaj9) and adding the scale's 9th to a minor chord creates a minor 9th (e.g., Cmin9).

Track 83

11th CHORDS

Adding an 11th to a chord is tricky because it often conflicts with the 3rd. For example, in F major if we try to create a dominant 11th (C11) the 11th is F, whereas the 3rd (the leading tone) is E. This sounds terrible for a number of reasons. First, they are a half step apart, the harshest dissonance in our system. Even if they are an octave apart, the minor 9th is nearly as dissonant. Then there is the problem that the E is supposed to "lead to" the tonic F, but that F is already sounding, which kills the feeling of progression. Finally, this is such a bad-sounding chord that it is virtually never used; it sounds strange to almost everyone. Instead of an 11th chord, we typically substitute a chord without the 3rd, most commonly a "sus4" chord that contains the 11th (here named 4, again because the octave it appears in does not matter). The "sus" part is for "suspended," meaning that, in theory at least, it is held over from the previous chord until it resolves to E, which it may or may not do. (See Appendix E for more on suspensions.)

Another substitute for the true 11th chord omits the 3rd and 5th, but adds in the 9th – in the key of F, for example, the note D. The notes C-Bb-D-F form what is often called Bb/C or "Bb with a C bass." It has the same function and affect as C11. These substitutes sound so good that they are often used; you are probably familiar with their sounds already.

13th CHORDS

The last note we can add is a 13th. This is a dominant chord common in jazz, occasionally used in other genres. It is almost always used as a dominant. The 13th is rarely altered because the #13 is the same sound as the minor 7th, while the b13 sounds like a raised 5th.

If the 13th is included in a triad without the 7th, we end up with a 6th chord, as in C6. Using a 6th abandons the "stack of 3rds" concept, as does using any even-numbered member of the scale. If we decide to stack the notes of C6, we end up with the same notes as Am7. These two different chords are made up of the same notes; it is the bass that determines which name to use, as well as the function of the chord. It may be interesting to see that the 6th added to the tonic produces the 7th chord of the relative minor – i.e., C6 has the same notes as Am7.

 Track 86

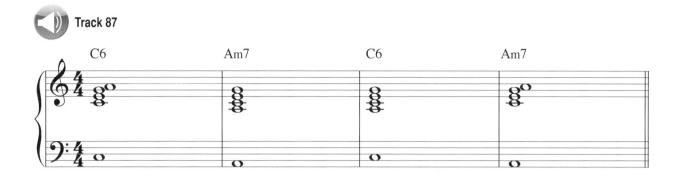

COMBINATIONS

Some chords combine added members to make more complex-sounding names, but often great sounds. A C6/9 chord is one example. It adds a major 6th and a major 9th to a C major chord for a fantastic sound that takes you back to some great 1930s jazz. More recently, Laurence Juber made great use of these chords on "Maple Avenue Strut" on his *Wooden Horses* (2009) album.

QUARTAL HARMONY

You might notice that all the notes in the C6/9 chord (except the root) form a stack of 4ths, which is part of the chord's interesting sound. Chords based on the interval of a 4th are sometimes used, but are beyond the scope of an introduction such as this. I do not recommend using them in your first song.

CADENCE TYPES

Musical cadences are points of division in a song, like punctuation in writing. They can be full cadences (or perfect cadences) like the period or full stop, or they can be half cadences, more like commas as the melodic sense continues.

Here, we'll describe the different cadence types in detail. This is not meant to be a compose-by-the-numbers type of automatic song generator. I hope it will help you understand what you have written, and perhaps fix spots you are not satisfied with, but cannot say exactly why. Our ears have developed certain expectations we can play with by fulfilling, not fulfilling, or delaying fulfillment. Before we can do any of these, though, we need to know what those expectations are.

Most of what follows comes from observation over centuries; some of it has been solidified into "rules" by various teachers and traditions. The fact that different traditions have different rules, even within the same genre, indicates that you should take any rule with a grain of salt, and trust your ear more than any book. (Yes, that includes this one).

FULL CADENCE

A full cadence is defined by the presence of a V-I or V7-I progression at the end of a melodic statement such as the end of a verse, a chorus, or any important section of a song. This has a conclusive sound and leaves no doubt in a listener's mind that this section has ended. Too many of these give a song a jerky, start-stop sound.

Classical music theory defines several sub-types of the full cadence (perfect cadence) based on the movement of the melody – and, to some extent, the movement of the bass as well. While it is not important to know the names, the ideas behind them can make a big difference in your writing. Let's look at the implications of the *melody* note you end on.

Ending on the tonic note gives a terminal feel to the cadence; this is best saved for the very end. However, it can be used in the middle of a song if you want to have a sudden complete stop for musical reasons. Because the leading tone moves up to the tonic so strongly, we feel that pull toward complete resolution. (See Example A on page 98.)

Approaching the tonic note from the note above it is almost as strong an ending, since that note seems to "relax" down into the tonic to end the phrase. (See Example.) Leaping to the tonic note from another note is less effective (such as from the root of the dominant chord).

Notice that the chord progression can be V-I or V7-I. Either is a full cadence.

Ending on the 3rd of the tonic chord is a less conclusive ending. Because the melody has not stopped on the tonic note, the last bar is not as stable as it could be, and our ear hears that. This makes it easier to continue on. This is useful – from ending a verse that continues on into another verse, to ending a movement of a symphony that has several more movements to go. (Listen to Beethoven's symphonies and hear how often movements other than the last one end on the 3rd of the tonic chord.) This movement can be strengthened by approaching the 3rd of the tonic from the 7th of the V7 chord, as shown in Example C. The final note sounds more inevitable because it resolves the 7th, and yet it is not as final as the tonic note. This can be used to make a softer ending to a song, or to a section.

The 3rd of the tonic does not need to follow the 7th of the V7, but can smoothly come from the 5th (D in our C major example) if you like. Skipping to it from the leading tone sounds wrong; unless you find an unusual use that you like, it is better avoided. You could also leap to it from the root of the V chord, which gives a more unexpected sound.

Ending on the 5th of the tonic chord allows you to use the same melody note for the whole full cadence. This has a unique sound that can be quite compelling; try it out for yourself, singing the melody and playing simple chords under your voice. It works well with either V-I or V7-I. The 5th is decidedly resonant, and this accounts for a large part of the effect, but the repetition of the note is important, too. (See Example D below.)

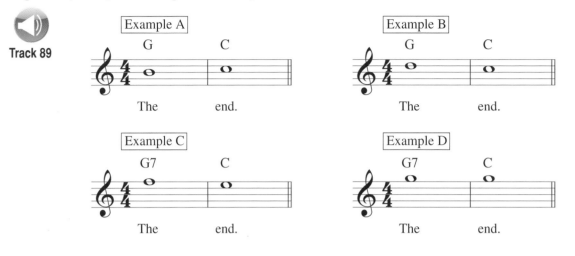

The other options for ending on the 5th of the tonic are poor in comparison. Leaping from the leading tone to the 5th of the tonic chord sounds odd and incomplete. Leaping from the 5th of the V to the 5th of the I gives a hollow parallel sound that you should avoid unless you find it appealing. (This is the "forbidden" parallel 5th of classical theory that classical composers strictly avoided, except when they didn't. That rather weak joke is actually true; almost all classical composers tended to avoid parallel 5ths, yet you can find at least a couple in almost any composer's work.)

The second-best approach to the 5th of the tonic chord is from the 7th of V7. Since the ear expects this note to resolve downward, the rise is a surprise and yet the result is resonant enough for the ear to accept it. It has a "struggle" type of sound, as if the last note breaks free from the expected resolution. This can be especially effective if the words reflect that feeling as well.

The bass motion in a full cadence is an important consideration. Even though our objective here is to write songs in lead sheet format where the chord is indicated just by name, there is a big difference in the sound of G7-C and G7/B-C. (G7/B means a G7 chord with B in the bass.) Since the strongest bass motion is a descending 5th (or an ascending 4th – either one here is G-C), having the V or V7 chord in root position makes the chord progression a strong ending. A weaker bass movement, from the leading tone or the 5th of V7, makes the cadence weaker as well, a less definite stop. A leap from the 7th of V7 to the root of the tonic chord sounds inconclusive – if not plain wrong.

If the tonic chord does not have its root in the bass, the cadence feels incomplete, as if you did not end a sentence quite as you meant. More advanced composers might use the 7th of V7 in the bass going to the 3rd of the tonic chord in the bass, but this is beyond the scope of this particular book.

DECEPTIVE CADENCE

A deceptive cadence seems to be one kind, but changes at the last chord, surprising the listener with a sonority they did not expect. Let's look at the most common type of deception, in which a V7 chord does not lead to I at the end of a phrase where we are expecting it. By far the most common deceptive cadence is V-vi or V7-vi. In our C major examples this is G-Am or G7-Am.

Track 90

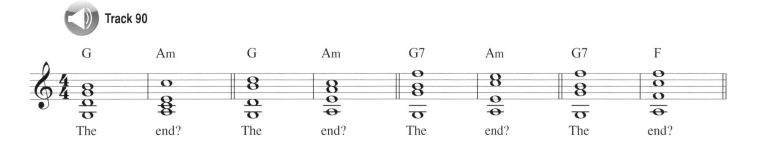

Since the notes C and E are common to both C major and A minor triads, the deception is the change of bass note from the expected C to A. If necessary, any Gs that might have been in the C chord are now As as well, although it is most common to see only the notes C and E above the A bass (as in the first and third examples above).

Most of the action in a deceptive cadence is in the bass, so simply writing a vi chord instead of a I chord above the last note creates the deception. If you are using G7 as the penultimate chord, it is possible to have the same note in the melody by not resolving the 7th of the V7 chord but holding it over to become the root of the IV chord, as shown in the last example above. For this to work, the F chord must have A as its bass note. This is a first-inversion triad, usually written as F/A in a lead sheet. In this case, the bass note is crucial to achieving the effect and must be notated.

Deceptive cadences are also effective in minor keys. Whereas part of the surprise in a major key is that the deceptive chord is minor, in a minor key the deceptive chord is major:

Track 91

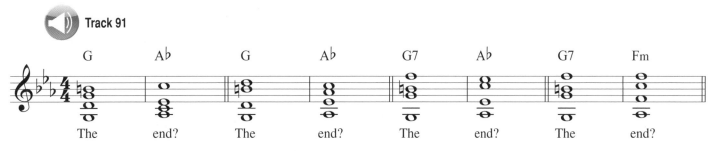

Typical uses of a deceptive cadence include avoiding a strong ending to a section and its opposite, strengthening the ending by seeming to avoid it, only to circle around again and this time end more strongly.

Track 92

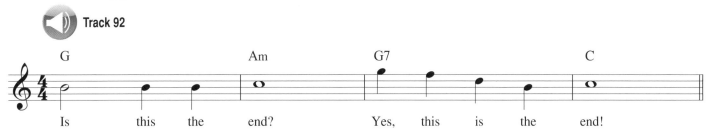

In a fuller context, we could change the last verse of "Amazing Grace" by adding a deceptive cadence to what seems the end of the song, followed by the true ending. You will most likely recognize this device immediately. This type of cadence allows us to repeat a lyric and add extra emphasis to the second time without changing the melody.

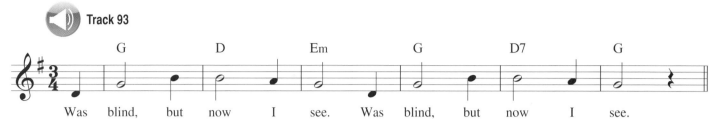

Tierce de Picardie

A Tierce de Picardie is simply the raised 3rd degree of the tonic chord at the end of a song in minor. The term sounds more impressive in French, translating simply as "Picardy 3rd" and indicating where it was supposedly first used. In any case, concluding a song in minor with a major tonic is a strong ending, although it has been used so often that it might be considered overused. It has become a cliché, but like most clichés it can still be striking if used sparingly.

HALF CADENCE

A half cadence is a sort of soft subdivision of a melody, one that works like a comma to separate sections and allow for a breath to be taken. The harmonic component is a chord progression that needs continuation since it is incomplete. This means that a half cadence will not end on the tonic chord.

The simplest type of half cadence is I-V. Sounding the tonic chord before the dominant reminds our ears that we have not come to rest on the tonic. A stronger half cadence is IV-V, which emphasizes the need to continue harmonically. While theoretically almost any chord moving to V can form a half cadence, I-V and IV-V are almost always chosen, although sometimes ii-V or vi-V are used as well. The V chord is used in preference to the V7, since V7 has a restless quality that undercuts the idea of a rest, however short.

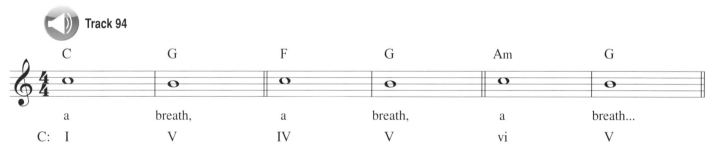

Having the melody pause on the leading tone emphasizes the need to continue melodically. Any other melodic choice is more subtle.

NON-CHORD TONES

While chord tones in a melody are the link to the backing harmony, a melody made up only of chord tones is just a series of broken chords or arpeggios. A typical melody contains mostly scale-like passages with occasional leaps, so there must be ways to join chord tones into this type of passage. Here we discuss the most common types of non-chord tones. It's important that you know how to use these in your own melodies; don't be too concerned about the specific names of each.

PASSING TONES

Passing tones are notes that move from one chord tone to another. Since chords are usually triads, there is a single passing tone between most chord members, specifically between the root and the 3rd, and between the 3rd and the 5th.

If we use triads, there is a larger space between the 5th of the chord and the root above it than between the other notes in the chord. This is the interval of a 4th; it requires two passing tones between the 5th and upper root.

Track 95

We call this type of passing tone *diatonic* because the notes we are using are those of the key. There are also *chromatic* passing tones, which use all the half steps between chord members, regardless of the key. By convention, we use sharps when ascending, and flats when descending.

Track 96

Notice that between major 3rds there are three chromatic passing tones, while between minor 3rds there are only two.

NEIGHBOR NOTES

Neighbor notes are immediately above or below a chord tone. They return to the chord tone from which they came. That's what makes them different from passing tones. Again, they can be diatonic or chromatic.

🔊 Track 97

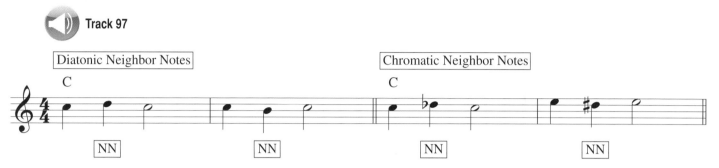

In the last bar, we used E instead of C to demonstrate the lower chromatic neighbor note since the B a half step below C is part of the C major scale (and thus is a diatonic neighbor note).

APPOGGIATURAS

Appoggiaturas are notes that appear on accented beats but are not chord tones. These "leaning tones" create tension that is released when they resolve to a chord tone as the next note. The effect is strongest when the note is dissonant with the chord, but they can also be convincing when used subtly. They should proceed logically from the melody; otherwise, they may sound like a wrong note.

🔊 Track 98

SUSPENSIONS

A suspension is a note held from one chord into the next. The held note can be common to both chords, or it can be dissonant with the second chord. In that case, it acts like an appoggiatura and resolves into a chord tone.

I chose the last example of an appoggiatura to demonstrate a problem with the idea of "suspension" in the harmony of popular music. Many would call the G chord with the C in the melody a Gsus4 chord. Technically, they are right. The note C does occur in the C major chord the bar before, even though it is not the melodic tone; if we consider that the C is held over from some other "voice" in that chord, then it is a suspension. Even if you have not studied harmony, you can probably tell that this is a bit of a stretch. Most people would omit the B from the G major chord when they heard how awful it sounds against the C in the melody; they would be left with the chord G–C–D, which they have learned to label a Gsus4 chord. You can too if you like, but keep in mind that the concept of suspension really applies to your melody; it is there that it is important to be clear about it. It can be effective to hold a long melody note into a chord where it becomes dissonant, and then finally resolve it to a chord tone. This is one of those cases where you have to trust your ears rather than your eyes. If you look at the lead sheet, you might see that your held note doesn't fit the new chord, but if you sing it with the chord and resolve it properly, it might sound great.

Suspensions usually resolve down, to the chord tone below them. As always, this is not an absolute rule. Sometimes, resolving up can give an unexpected but good effect. This is especially true if the note resolves up a half step. When in doubt, or if it just doesn't sound right, resolve a suspension down.

Track 99

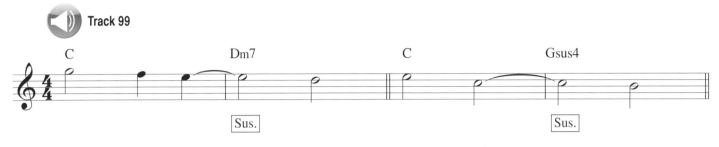

Next we have double suspensions (one of the tied notes is part of the next chord) where C is held as the bass goes to D in the first example, and G in the second. Sometimes complex names are used for these chords, but they are just suspensions:

Track 100

For comparison, here are two suspensions that resolve upward. Compare the first example with the one above and see which your ear prefers. In the example where we suspend the note B from the G chord into the C following, notice the effect of delayed resolution of the leading tone. You will hear this as an ending to some songs, as if the singer were reluctant to finish with that last note.

Track 101

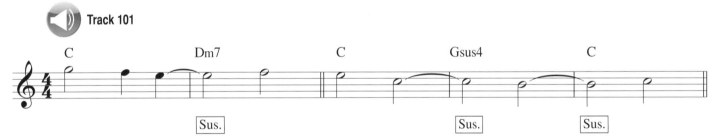

ANTICIPATIONS

Don't confuse anticipations with suspensions. Anticipations are notes that appear before they "should" appear according to the harmony; they are not part of the chord they appear with. They give a sense of urgency or stress to the note they anticipate. Any note can be anticipated, but it is usually in the melody.

Track 102

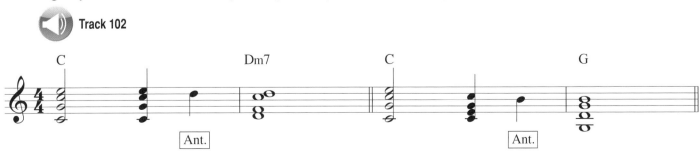

Writing music is encoding it in a type of notation designed by musicians to communicate with other musicians; reading it is decoding the music from that notation. Over the centuries it took to develop, notation first showed the general direction of a melody, then actual pitches; it moved on to add rhythms and finally more and more precise directions on how to play the music. This last part is in some ways the breakdown in the system, because pitch and rhythm are encoded independent of any spoken language. As soon as composers wanted to add the feeling that the notes were meant to evoke, or more precise or semi-precise directions (e.g., "with fire"), they had to resort to a particular language. At first it was Italian, in which it is easy to learn the few words needed for music. However, with the nationalistic feelings that arose during the 16th to 20th centuries, directions began to be written in French, German, English, and other languages native to the composers.

Here we'll concentrate on the most important features of notation – pitch and rhythm – the same elements that require no knowledge of any particular spoken language. We begin by decoding one note at a time. As we get better at it, we start to recognize patterns we've seen before, such as scales or broken chords. Like most things, it improves with practice. Rhythm is similar.

Pitch notation employs a staff of five lines. We use both the lines and spaces between them to place notes. The higher on the staff, the higher their pitch sounds. In the example below, we have the letter name of each note inside it, starting with "middle C" (which will be explained soon). The pattern is simple enough: We use the letters from A to G and then start over again, so there are only seven letter names to learn.

Track 103

Middle C

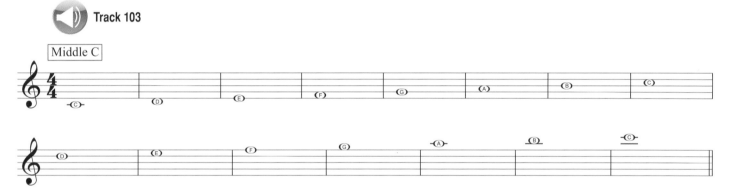

In the last three bars we needed to show notes that were higher than the staff allowed, so we added extra lines (called "ledger lines") and used them and the spaces above them, as necessary. These are not part of the staff; they are used only for the notes that need them.

The notes on each line are three note names from the line above or below, counting the name of that other line as well, which music theory calls a 3rd. Because our harmonic system is made up of chords built from 3rds, we can construct these chords simply by using notes on consecutive lines or consecutive spaces. This is the basis of Appendix C, Triadic Harmony.

The treble clef is most often used to notate melodies, but there are several other clefs, the most common of which is the bass clef. Combining the treble and bass clefs gives us the "grand staff," which is most commonly used for piano music. Thus "middle C" is the note between the two staves. Since neither staff includes this note, we need a ledger line to show it in either one.

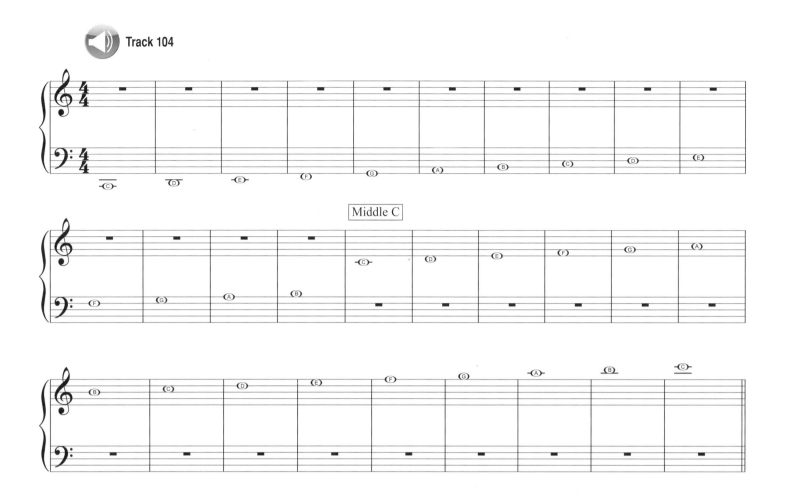

Middle C

A handy piece of information is that the guitar, bass, and bass guitar sound an octave below the pitch written on the staff, just as the tenor voice does. Although the guitar is written in the treble clef, its notes sound more in the bass range. For example, the second-string first-fret note C sounds like middle C played on the piano (which sounds just as it is written). The open G string on a bass, written in the top space of the bass clef, sounds like the G on the lowest line of the bass clef. Instruments that sound notes differently from the way they are written on the staff are called "transposing instruments," while instruments like the piano that sound at notated pitch are called "non-transposing instruments."

The notes in the preceding examples are from the C major scale. On the piano, they consist of only the white keys. Obviously, these are not all the possible notes, because a piano has black keys as well (and if you play the C major scale on the guitar, you will see that you do not use every fret), but they do use all the letter names. We notate the other pitches by raising or lowering the regular letter names, using a sharp (♯) to raise a note a half step (or one fret) and a flat (♭) to lower a half step. In the rare instances it is necessary to raise or lower two half steps, we use a double-sharp (✗) or double-flat (♭♭).

A quirk of either the notational system or our major scales is that not every note is an equal distance from its neighbors. While most notes in the C major scale are a whole step (or two half steps or two frets) apart, there are two exceptions that are just one fret distant: E-F and B-C. Of course, using sharps and flats also changes the distances, so while E-F is a half step, E-F♯ is two half steps or a whole step, while B♭-C is also a whole step.

This is the basis for decoding pitch from written music. Study the Rhythm chapter and, with some work, you will be able to read and write basic music notation.

ACKNOWLEDGMENTS

This book is dedicated to my wife Laurie, who believed in me even when I didn't. Her love and support have sustained me through much worse than writing a book, but her belief in me is what started the whole project. If this book helps you, thank her; if not, blame me.

I could not have finished this book without the support of my good friend Don Lococo. We are all fortunate if we can make good friendships that last a lifetime and I was lucky enough to meet Don on the first day of high school. He was wise enough to talk with me about anything except songwriting.

I am deeply grateful for the support of my dear friend Margaret Markham, for her compassion as well as her inspiration as an artist.

I cannot adequately thank Dr. Angela Jones for keeping me alive long enough to write this book. I also owe a huge debt to Dr. Jay Stewart and Mari-Lou Jorgenson, who were key in my recovery. And thanks to my friend John Knowles for his wise counsel and support over many years.

At Hal Leonard Corporation, I have to thank Jeff Schroedl for green-lighting the project and for answering innumerable emails, as well as his personal support, which I appreciate even more. Also my thanks to Lori Hagopian for encouraging me to submit ideas in the first place and for putting me in touch with Jeff. My deep and sincerest thanks to J. Mark Baker for his careful editing and tightening up of my sometimes rambling text. Every reader will benefit from his sharp eyes and his ability to get right to the point. I would thank him more effusively, but then he'd cut that part anyway.

Finally, I need to apologize to Neil Peart of Rush for not getting the rights to use his words to "Limelight" as a Preface to this book. The whole song expresses the spirit of the book, as those of you who know the lyrics will readily recognize. If you are not familiar with this great example of songwriting, I highly encourage you to download it (legally) and do yourself a big favor.

ABOUT THE AUTHOR

Dr. Dave Walker has been teaching music theory, songwriting, and guitar for over 40 years. After an Honours Mus.Bac. in Composition at the University of Toronto he completed a Master of Science in Computer Science (specializing in MIDI) and then a Master of Arts in Music. He holds a triple-specialty PhD in Education, Computing, and Music from the University of Toronto and has taught in universities and colleges throughout Ontario. He continues to perform and produce, and writes music that ranges from full symphonic scores to songs, in small combo and solo arrangements.

Dr. Walker has recorded several video courses, most recently on music theory for beginners, has run two successful websites devoted to music theory and introducing new artists, and has written dozens of articles ranging from academic subjects to artist interviews and product reviews. He was an innovator in the field of multimedia applications, giving invited talks on his work at Harvard, Yale, CUNY graduate school, the University of Osnabrück (Germany), and several schools in his native Canada. After creating many more multimedia teaching applications, Dave was promoted to Director of Learning Technologies, but still found time to teach music theory in the graduate school as well running his private studio. After several teaching awards, he seized the opportunity for early retirement, allowing him to concentrate exclusively on music and expand his work with coaching songwriters from beginners to pros. A room full of CDs testifies to his wide range of work. He has performed his own songs and arrangements from Toronto to Nashville, often with his own students, many of whom have gone on to university or professional careers. For the past seven years he has reached a wider audience as a writer and reviewer, often for *Just Jazz Guitar* magazine, where he writes articles as well as two regular columns, "On Music Theory" and "Music Software."

Although Dave continues to write both classical and popular music, he says that his greatest joy now is to help others to express themselves. "Seeing the sense of accomplishment and pride on a new songwriter's face is one of the most touching experiences I have ever had. I have tried to put all I have learned over the years – from my many students as much as from my teachers – into this book. My only regret is that I will not be there to witness the reader's transformation into a songwriter."

How To...

This series gives musicians the skinny on a wide variety of topics. Written by different authors with specific expertise, each title delves deep into the subject, getting readers started on the skills they're most interested in.

GUITAR BOOKS

How to Build Guitar Chops
by Chad Johnson
00147679 Book/Online Audio $16.99

How to Enjoy Guitar with Just 3 Chords
by David Harrison
00288990 Book Only................................$7.99

How to Fingerpick Songs on Guitar
by Chad Johnson
00155364 Book/Online Video.................$14.99

How to Get Better at Guitar
by Thorsten Kober
00157666 Book/Online Audio................$19.99

How to Play Blues-Fusion Guitar
by Joe Charupakorn
00137813 Book/Online Audio................$19.99

How to Play Blues/Rock Guitar Solos
by David Grissom
00249561 Book/Online Audio................$16.99

How to Play Boogie Woogie Guitar
by Dave Rubin
00157974 Book/Online Video.................$14.99

How to Play Country Lead Guitar
by Jeff Adams
00131103 Book/Online Audio................$19.99

How to Play Outside Guitar Licks
by Chris Buono
00140855 Book/Online Video................$19.99

How to Play Rock Lead Guitar
by Brooke St. James
00146260 Book/Online Video.................$14.99

How to Play Rock Rhythm Guitar
by Brooke St. James
00146261 Book/Online Video.................$14.99

How to Strum Chords on Guitar
by Burgess Speed
00154902 Book/Online Video.................$14.99

BASS BOOKS

How to Create Rock Bass Lines
by Steve Gorenberg
00151784 Book/Online Audio................$16.99

How to Play Blues Bass
by Mark Epstein
00260179 Book/Online Audio................$14.99

DRUM BOOKS

How to Build Drum Grooves Over Bass Lines
by Alan Arber
00287564 Book/Online Audio................$16.99

How to Play Rock Drums
by David Lewitt
00138541 Book/Online Audio................$16.99

PIANO/KEYBOARD BOOKS

How to Play Blues Piano by Ear
by Todd Lowry
00121704 Book/Online Audio................$16.99

How to Play Boogie Woogie Piano
by Arthur Migliazza & Dave Rubin
00140698 Book/Online Audio................$16.99

How to Play R&B Soul Keyboards
by Henry Brewer
00232890 Book/Online Audio................$16.99

How to Play Solo Jazz Piano
by John Valerio
00147731 Book/Online Audio................$16.99

STRINGS BOOK

How to Play Contemporary Strings
by Julie Lyonn Lieberman
00151259 Book/Online Media................$16.99

UKULELE BOOK

How to Play Solo Ukulele
by Chad Johnson
00159809 Book/Online Audio................$16.99

VOCAL BOOK

How to Sight Sing
by Chad Johnson
00156132 Book/Online Audio................$16.99

OTHER VOLUMES

How to Improvise Over Chord Changes
by Shawn Wallace, Dr. Keith Newton, Kris Johnson & Steve Kortyka
00138009 Book Only................................$24.99

How to Read Music
by Mark Phillips
00137870 Book Only..................................$9.99

How to Record at Home on a Budget
by Chad Johnson
00131211 Book/Online Audio................$19.99

How to Write Your First Song
by Dave Walker
00138010 Book/Online Audio................$16.99

HAL•LEONARD®
www.halleonard.com

MUSIC BUSINESS MUST-HAVES

ALL YOU NEED TO KNOW ABOUT THE MUSIC BUSINESS – 8TH EDITION
by Donald S. Passman
Free Press

The definitive and essential guide to the music industry, now in its eighth edition – revised and updated with crucial information on the industry's major changes in response to rapid technological advances and economic uncertainty.
00119121 ....$32.00

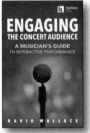

ENGAGING THE CONCERT AUDIENCE
by David Wallace
Berklee Press

Learn to engage, excite, captivate and expand your audience! These practical techniques will help you to communicate with your listeners on a deeper, more interactive level. As you do, the concert experience will become more meaningful, and the bond between you and your audience will grow.
00244532 Book/Online Media $16.99

HOW TO GET A JOB IN THE MUSIC INDUSTRY – 3RD EDITION
by Keith Hatschek with Breanne Beseda
Berklee Press

This third edition includes a new career tool kit and social media strategy. Inside you'll find: details on booming job prospects in digital music distribution and music licensing; interviews with nine music industry professionals under 35 who discuss how they got their starts, plus what skills today's leading job candidates must possess; and much more.
00130699 ....$27.99

MANAGING YOUR BAND – SIXTH EDITION
ARTIST MANAGEMENT: THE ULTIMATE RESPONSIBILITY
by Stephen Marcone with David Philp

From dive bars to festivals, from branding and merchandising to marketing and publicity, from publishing and licensing to rights and contracts, Marcone and Philp leave no stone unturned in this comprehensive guide to artist management.
00200476 ....$34.95

MELODY IN SONGWRITING
by Jack Perricone
Berklee Press

Discover songwriting techniques from the hit makers! This comprehensive guide unlocks the secrets of hit songs, examining them, and revealing why they succeed. Learn to write memorable melodies and discover the dynamic relationships between melody, harmony, rhythm, and rhyme.
50449419 ....$24.99

MUSIC LAW IN THE DIGITAL AGE – 2ND EDITION
by Allen Bargfrede
Berklee Press

With the free-form exchange of music files and musical ideas online, understanding copyright laws has become essential to career success in the new music marketplace. This cutting-edge, plain-language guide shows you how copyright law drives the contemporary music industry.
00148196 ....$19.99

MUSIC MARKETING FOR THE DIY MUSICIAN
by Bobby Borg
Music Pro Guides
Music Marketing for the DIY Musician is a proactive, practical, step-by-step guide to producing a fully integrated, customized, low-budget plan of attack for artists marketing their own music.
00124611 ....$29.99

MUSIC MARKETING
by Mike King
Berklee Press

Sell more music! Learn the most effective marketing strategies available to musicians, leveraging the important changes and opportunities that the digital age has brought to music marketing. This multifaceted and integrated approach will help you to develop an effective worldwide marketing strategy.
50449588 ....$24.99

PAT PATTISON'S SONGWRITING: ESSENTIAL GUIDE TO RHYMING – 2ND EDITION
Berklee Press

If you have written lyrics before, even at a professional level, you can still gain greater control and understanding of your craft with the exercises and worksheets included in this book. Hone your writing technique and skill with this practical and fun approach to the art of lyric writing.
00124366 ....$17.99

THE PLAIN AND SIMPLE GUIDE TO MUSIC PUBLISHING – 3RD EDITION
by Randall D. Wixen

In this expanded and updated third edition, Randall D. Wixen adds greater depth to such increasingly important topics as the rapidly shifting industry paradigms, the growing importance of streaming and subscription models, a discussion of new compulsary license media, and so much more.
00122219 ....$24.99

SONGWRITING: ESSENTIAL GUIDE TO LYRIC FORM AND STRUCTURE
by Pat Pattison
Berklee Press

Veteran songwriter Pat Pattison has taught many of Berklee College of Music's best and brightest students how to write truly great lyrics. Her helpful guide contains essential information on lyric structures, timing and placement, and exercises to help everyone from beginners to seasoned songwriters say things more effectively and gain a better understanding of their craft.
50481582 ....$16.99

SONGWRITING STRATEGIES
by Mark Simos
Berklee Press

Write songs starting from any direction: melody, lyric, harmony, rhythm, or idea. This book will help you expand your range and flexibility as a songwriter. Discussions, hands-on exercises, and notated examples will help you hone your craft. This creatively liberating approach supports the overall integrity of emotion and meaning in your songs.
50449621 ....$24.99

HAL•LEONARD®
www.halleonard.com